D1109977

By Fisher Howe:

The Board Member's Guide to Fund Raising

Welcome to the Board

Other books in the Jossey-Bass Nonprofit Sector Series:

Achieving Excellence in Fund Raising, *Henry A. Rosso and Associates*

Board Leadership: A Bimonthly Workshop with John Carver

Board Overboard, *Brian O'Connell*

Boards That Make a Difference, 2nd Edition, *John Carver*

Building an Effective Nonprofit Board (audio), *National Center for Nonprofit Boards*

The CarverGuide Series on Effective Board Governance, *John Carver*

John Carver on Board Governance (video), *John Carver*

The Drucker Foundation Self-Assessment Tool for Nonprofit Organizations, *The Peter F. Drucker Foundation for Nonprofit Management*

Executive Leadership in Nonprofit Organizations, *Robert D. Herman, Richard D. Heimovics*

Governing Boards, Revised Edition, *Cyril O. Houle*

The Jossey-Bass Handbook of Nonprofit Leadership and Management, *Robert D. Herman and Associates*

The Leader of the Future, *Frances Hesselbein, Marshall Goldsmith, Richard Beckhard, Editors*

Leader to Leader (quarterly), *The Peter F. Drucker Foundation for Nonprofit Management*

Making Boards Effective, *Alvin Zander*

Managing for Accountability, *Kevin Kearns*

Marketing Nonprofit Programs and Services, *Douglas B. Herron*

Nonprofit Boards and Leadership, *Miriam M. Wood, Editor*

Nonprofit Management and Leadership (quarterly)

The Organization of the Future, *Frances Hesselbein, Marshall Goldsmith, Richard Beckhard, Editors*

Pathways to Leadership, *James Lawrence Powell*

The Board Member's Guide
to Strategic Planning

National Center for Nonprofit Boards

The mission of the National Center for Nonprofit Boards (NCNB) is to improve the effectiveness of the more than one million nonprofit organizations throughout the United States by strengthening their boards of directors.

To carry out its mission, NCNB:

- Publishes booklets and other resources, including books, videos, audiotapes, and computer diskettes, to help strengthen board performance. Nonprofit leaders have purchased more than 450,000 copies of these materials, making NCNB the world's largest publisher and distributor of information for nonprofit boards.

- Conducts workshops, conferences, and other training programs, including an annual National Leadership Forum, local and regional workshops throughout the country, interactive satellite television broadcasts, and tailored board development programs.

- Provides information and advice to thousands of nonprofit leaders, journalists, educators, and others who write, call, fax, or e-mail the Board Information Center each year.

- Offers membership to board members, chief executives, and other nonprofit leaders. Members receive a subscription to NCNB's periodical, *Board Member*; substantial discounts on NCNB resources and services; and opportunities for networking and sharing information.

- Works with partner organizations outside the United States to increase the capacity for board training and development and to strengthen the boards of civil society organizations throughout the world.

Established in 1988 by the Association of Governing Boards of Universities and Colleges (AGB) and INDEPENDENT SECTOR, the National Center for Nonprofit Boards is a 501(c)(3) nonprofit organization. NCNB received a lead grant from the W.K. Kellogg Foundation and continues to receive grants from corporations, foundations, and individuals. Income from the sale of publications, fees for meetings and training programs, and membership dues are also important sources of financial support.

For more information, contact:

**NATIONAL
CENTER FOR
NONPROFIT
BOARDS**

Suite 510
2000 L Street, NW
Washington, DC
20036–4907

Tel. 202–452–6262
Fax 202–452–6299
ncnb@ncnb.org

The Board Member's Guide to Strategic Planning

A Practical Approach to Strengthening Nonprofit Organizations

Fisher Howe

Foreword by Howard H. Williams III

A publication of the
National Center for Nonprofit Boards

Jossey-Bass Publishers
San Francisco

Copyright © 1997 by Jossey-Bass Inc., Publishers, 350 Sansome Street, San Francisco, California 94104.

All rights reserved. No part of this publication may be reproduced, stored in a retrieval system, or transmitted, in any form or by any means, electronic, mechanical, photocopying, recording, or otherwise, without the prior written permission of the publisher.

Substantial discounts on bulk quantities of Jossey-Bass books are available to corporations, professional associations, and other organizations. For details and discount information, contact the special sales department at Jossey-Bass Inc., Publishers (415) 433–1740; Fax (800) 605–2665.

Jossey-Bass Web address: http://www.josseybass.com

 Manufactured in the United States of America on Lyons Falls Turin Book. This paper is acid-free and 100 percent totally chlorine-free.

In Chapter Ten, the principles of the American Association of Museums that the Pilgrim Society draws on for its fundamental values are reprinted with the permission of the American Association of Museums.

Also in Chapter Ten, the list of beliefs and values that Peter D. Relic, president of the National Association of Independent Schools, looks for in the schools he visits is reprinted with his permission.

In Chapter Twelve, the list of critical issues for strategic planning is from the *Strategic Planning Workbook for Nonprofit Organizations* by Bryan Barry. Copyright 1986. Reprinted by permission from the Amherst H. Wilder Foundation.

Library of Congress Cataloging-in-Publication Data

Howe, Fisher, date.
    The board member's guide to strategic planning : a practical
approach to strengthening nonprofit organizations / Fisher Howe ;
foreword by Howard H. Williams III.
        p.   cm. — (The Jossey-Bass nonprofit sector series)
    "A publication of the National Center for Nonprofit Boards."
    Includes bibliographical references and index.
    ISBN 0–7879–0825–8 (acid-free paper)
    1. Nonprofit organizations—Management.   2. Strategic planning.
3. Directors of corporations.   I. Title.   II. Series.
HD62.6.H693   1997
658.4'012—dc21   96–45898

HB Printing   10 9 8 7 6 5 4 3   FIRST EDITION

The Jossey-Bass Nonprofit Sector Series

Contents

Foreword

While I was reading this book, an unoriginal thought occurred to me: learning to plan is a lot like learning to ride a bicycle. You can read all you like and be told all you can bear, and all of that is helpful, of course, toward knowing what to do. But until you actually get on the bike and feel the inertia, the gravity, the forces—and the fall—you will never be a rider. You can read *this* book and know what to do and even how to do it. But until you set out and fall and do it again and finally succeed, you will never be a planner.

Fisher Howe knows these things full well. In *The Board Member's Guide to Strategic Planning* he sympathetically yet forcefully puts forth his ideas, inexorably driving the reader toward recognition of the inevitability and the verities of planning. Two objectives of the book are very clear. First, it is imperative that nonprofits devote more serious, purposeful attention to strategic planning, because the changing world is imposing increasingly harsher terms on nonprofits, to which they must respond. Second, there is a world of knowledge out there, and Fisher Howe has synthesized his message from that world—with considerable credit given to the many authors he references.

Howe draws on his extensive experience to articulate and season his thoughts. One of the more compelling aspects of this book is its rich use of examples from real-life nonprofits with which the author has been associated. Each story is different, at least in terms of situation, need, or capability. The sum of these parables, however, should convince all but the most hardened planning agnostic that assessing strategic needs and opportunities can be beneficial—and successful—for almost any organization. Howe shows how each board and/or executive staff—whether of a school, church, or care center—was able to define the need for attention and then convene the appropriate people to go through a process of rational debate to emerge with a consensus on aims and actions. As we know, this is no small accomplishment!

The ideas that Howe presents are particularly easy to follow, thanks not only to his direct language but also to the book's structure. As in the real world of strategy, the chapters describe and distinguish *what* from *how*. The *what* that should be planned is the beginning point. Clarity of purpose and expectation is crucial if planners are to avoid major disappointments. Then, as the book demonstrates, one can take up the question of *how* to go about the process of planning. Ample references and examples are provided for each aspect of the task.

One might choose to quibble with the author in one regard. It seems clear that planning efforts can be no better than the quality and capabilities of its participants—board leaders, senior staff, and facilitators. Howe addresses this point by suggesting judicious use of experienced outside consultants as substantive or process guides. Being a consultant myself, I know our limitations! So a board of trustees must be ever vigilant and carefully assess the logic and pragmatism of both the process and the plan. But if it happens to be true that the leaders of most nonprofits are like the farmer who, when advised by the county agent to improve his techniques, said, "I don't even farm now as well as I know how!" then great benefits can accrue simply by trying harder and by planning in a rational and committed manner.

I should admit, perhaps, that I know F. Howe, as he calls himself, and have considerable affection and admiration for him. Despite that bias, I will say that this book reflects three great characteristics of

the author: first, his zeal for nonprofits and for strategic planning—
you cannot miss the excitement and even the joy that accompany
his stories and ideas; second, his wisdom, which stems from years of
hands-on work in the field—one could learn a lot from his previous
books on the building of high-quality boards; and third, his good-
will and humor, which help to make a dry and sometimes forbid-
ding subject more accessible and attractive.

Howe has done us all a service. Let's make good use of it in our
own worlds.

Washington, D.C. Howard H. Williams III
December 1996 *Director, McKinsey and Company*
Chairman, Support Centers of America
Chairman, National Museum
*   of Natural History*
Vice Chair, Washington Home
*   Long-Term Care Center*

In memory of D.L.H.
brother, friend, teacher, masterful editor

Preface

The reason for this book is simple. Strategic planning is important to nonprofit organizations as a basis for strong *governance* by the board, sound *management* by the executive and staff, effective *fund raising* by both the board and the staff, and constructive *program evaluation* by all participants in fulfilling the organization's mission. Yet boards and staffs are notorious for avoiding strategic planning. "We are too busy doing our daily jobs to take time out to indulge in planning." "If anyone mentions strategic planning, I freeze up; I turn off." "Strategic planning exists to burnish the ego of the guru hired to put charts on the wall . . . for a price." "Strategic planning means making changes; why make changes when things are going so well?"

It need not be thus. Strategic planning need not be tedious, irrelevant, or expensive. On the contrary, it can be a process that arouses interest and enthusiasm. It can engender pride in the deliberate and rational performance of an organization. Strategic planning can be of enormous value to nonprofit organizations at different stages in their lives.

Many books are available on strategic planning. Few are written for board members; that is, few are brief enough to hold their attention, free enough of technical intricacies to be readily understood, and yet detailed enough to be practical.

In this book, the discussion of strategic planning is intended to encourage board members to participate, and to guide them in this activity that is so critical to organizational success. Executive directors and staffs who are introducing their boards to the concept of strategic planning should also find value in this book's message.

Let it be said at the outset: *The Board Member's Guide to Strategic Planning* does not seek to break new ground in the theories and techniques of strategic planning. It will not, as the academics say, "add to the literature." Its sole purpose is to be helpful to board members and executives who are considering the long-term outlook for their organization.

Every practitioner of strategic planning has a favorite formula, a pet process. No claim of uniqueness or superiority is made for the process set out here. The book is designed to suggest a straightforward, uncomplicated way of going about strategic planning. Organizations can follow, modify, or change this process to suit their own circumstances, whims, or prejudices—but still get on with the planning.

Nor is any claim made to originality. The philosophy, processes, and procedures of several masters of strategic planning are drawn upon liberally—shamelessly. They are noted and gratefully acknowledged.

I seem to have come to this subject naturally. In my book, *The Board Member's Guide to Fund Raising* (1991), I emphasized the need for strategic planning to achieve unambiguous statements of purposes, programs, and priorities, and to afford a firm basis for arriving at an estimate of the resources needed to support the organization. Similarly, my *Welcome to the Board: Your Guide to Effective Participation* (1995) featured the definition of purpose and mission as one of the seven responsibilities expected of a nonprofit board member, as well as periodic thorough strategic planning to review the mission and the programs designed to carry it out.

This book concentrates entirely on nonprofit organizations; it is not concerned with for-profit business planning, or with planning in public governmental agencies. Nonprofit organizations are those that are granted tax exemption by law, that meet the exemption requirements of the Internal Revenue Code or state statutes. While Section 501(c) of the Code lists twenty-five different types of such

organizations, for purposes of this discussion of strategic planning it
is helpful to distinguish only four types:

Public service organizations, including educational, health care,
cultural, community service, research, and advocacy organizations, which exist to provide services to the public

Membership organizations, including labor unions, professional
and trade associations, and community service associations,
which exist to serve their members

Grant-making organizations, notably foundations and United
Ways, which exist to provide funding support to other nonprofit organizations

Religious institutions, which are altogether distinctive, being in
essence membership organizations with an important public
service, spiritual mission

While the purposes of these types of nonprofit organizations may
vary, their approaches to strategic planning are essentially the same.
Aspects of institutional character—whether the institution is big
or small, new or old, national or local—will modify but not fundamentally change the process.

Overview of the Contents

The ultimate product of strategic planning is a *strategic plan*—
the board's determination of the guiding principles that govern the
activities of the organization—and an *operational plan*—the man-
ager's blueprint for implementation of the strategic plan. The
process of strategic planning, therefore, is the design for achieving
those products.

The chapters in Part One of the book seek to put into perspective the ways and means of strategic planning, including its benefits and the usual barriers that need to be overcome. The process of

strategic planning has two dimensions: *preparing* for strategic planning and *conducting* strategic planning. The chapters in Part Two take up the preparation—the organization and procedures, the design, the plans for planning, and the arrangements—while the chapters in Part Three address the content, the substance, of planning—how best to proceed down the logical path toward productive ends. The focus is on the mission, the values, the internal and external environments, and the critical issues, leading to the substantive outcome of the exercise—the vision of what the organization wants to be and do in the coming years. The chapters in Part Four describe the end products of strategic planning: the strategic and operational plans. Finally, the chapters in Part Five summarize the principles of successful planning. Parts Two, Three, and Four each end with a chapter that provides a list of *action steps* that can be used as a guide through that stage of the process.

At various places throughout the book, examples that illustrate a range of strategic planning experiences have been drawn, with their permission, from organizations with which I have been associated:

The Piedmont Environmental Council, Warrenton, Virginia: a regional land preservation and environmental advocacy organization

Hospice Care of D.C., Washington, D.C.: a community health care service

The Fountain Valley School, Colorado Springs, Colorado: an independent coeducational boarding and day school

Alzheimer's Association, Chicago: a national organization that supports medical research, with local chapters providing patient and home support

Pilgrim Society, Plymouth, Massachusetts: a museum and research institution

Grand Canyon Association, Arizona: a cooperative support organization for the national park

Grace Episcopal Church, Providence, Rhode Island: an established downtown city parish

National Society of Fund Raising Executives, Washington, D.C., chapter: a nonprofit professional association that serves its members

Gardner and Florence Call Cowles Foundation, Des Moines, Iowa: a fifty-year-old family grant-making foundation with assets of approximately $50 million.

Acknowledgments

I am greatly indebted to four authors who have brought special clarity to the subject of strategic planning, a subject too often submerged in confused rhetoric: the late Jonathan Cook, the founding director of the Support Centers of America, whose occasional papers were seminal contributions to the theories, practices, and language of planning; John M. Bryson, University of Minnesota professor, whose book *Strategic Planning for Public and Nonprofit Organizations* (1988) elucidates in detail the concepts, procedures, and tools of strategic planning, and whose insistence that a central benefit of strategic planning in forcing boards "to think strategically as never before and not be bound by present demands" is one of those simple but fundamental ideas too easily overlooked; John Carver, consultant to public, nonprofit, and business organizations, whose book *Boards That Make a Difference* brings important insights to strategic planning for nonprofit boards, especially the concept of *ends* and *means*; Dabney Park Jr., Florida consultant, who has led the way with his booklet *Strategic Planning and the Nonprofit Board* (1990), written for the National Center for Nonprofit Boards.

In preparing this manuscript I have also had invaluable direct assistance from many people. Those associated with the planning efforts cited in the illustrative examples have generously guided me in their descriptions of how they went about it: Michael Guthrie, board member of the Fountain Valley School; Charles Whitehouse, former president of the Piedmont Environmental Council; Christopher Hussey, president of the Pilgrim Society; Reverend Daniel Warren, rector of Grace Episcopal Church; Darla Scheuth, executive director of Hospice Care of D.C.; Robert Koons, president of the Grand Canyon Association; Ed Truschke, president of the Alzheimer's Association; Elizabeth Ballentine, board member of Gardner and Florence Call Cowles Foundation; and James Gelatt, former president of the D.C. chapter of the National Society of Fund Raising Executives.

My editor, Alan Shrader, was a constant guide, and the anonymous, highly professional "peer reviewers" he chose suggested both general and detailed ways to improve the manuscript. Former colleagues James Wickenden and Peter Szanton, practicing consultants, made helpful suggestions in response to the draft. So did my brother Lawrence Howe, of Chicago. A special note of appreciation goes to two lifetime friends who have been generous and merciless but always constructive in their criticism of draft chapters: Francis D. Moore, of Boston, and Charles F. Haas, of Studio City, California.

Washington, D.C.   Fisher Howe
December 1996

The Author

FISHER HOWE is a consultant for nonprofit organizations with the firm of Lavender/Howe & Associates, which has offices in Ojai, California, and Washington, D.C. Howe received his B.A. degree (1935) from Harvard University in history and literature and later had a full career in the Foreign Service. He has served as assistant dean and executive director at the Johns Hopkins University School of Advanced International Studies, and as director of institutional relations for Resources for the Future, a research organization for energy, natural resources, and the environment located in Washington, D.C.

Howe has been a trustee of several organizations, including the Fountain Valley School in Colorado Springs, Hospice Care of D.C., the Washington Area Council on Alcohol and Drug Abuse, the Metropolitan Washington United Way, the Institute for Circadian Physiology (Boston), the Support Center of Washington, the Pilgrim Society (Plymouth, Massachusetts), and the Washington chapter of the National Society of Fund Raising Executives. His publications include "What You Need to Know About Fund Raising," published in the *Harvard Business Review* (1986); "Fund Raising and the Nonprofit Board Member," (1988); *The Board Member's Guide to Fund Raising: What Every Trustee Needs to Know About Raising Money* (1991); and *Welcome to the Board: Your Guide to Effective Participation* (1995).

The Board Member's Guide
to Strategic Planning

Part I

The Board's Perspective
on Strategic Planning

1. *Benefits of Strategic Planning*
2. *The Board's Responsibility for Strategic Planning*
3. *Examples of Strategic Planning from the Board Perspective*
4. *The Language of Planning*

An orderly approach to the complex subject of strategic planning calls at the outset for a discussion of the whys and wherefores. Chapter One thus explores the various reasons, the stimulants, for organizations to undertake planning. Chapter Two points to where the responsibility for strategic planning lies: with the board. Chapter Three illustrates the reasons for planning and the assumption of responsibility through the experience of various organizations. Finally, Chapter Four makes explicit the rhetoric of strategic planning, which is steeped in special meanings.

Benefits of Strategic Planning

When you look at the benefits of strategic planning, you wonder why every institution doesn't put it at the top of its list. It seems so obvious.

Even when organizations accept in a general way the need for strategic planning, they tend to misunderstand just what such planning means and how to carry it out effectively. Decision making in organizations that exist to serve a public need can be less than crystal clear, and the environment in which such organizations operate is invariably complex. Planning is not easy.

In the simplest terms, an organization undertakes strategic planning to reaffirm or to modify its *mission*—why it exists, what its purpose is, and what it now does—and to agree on its *vision*—what it wants to *be* and *do* in the coming years. Strategic planning need not be more; it must not be less.

Bryson (1988) emphasizes that "a strategic planning process is merely a way of helping key decision makers think and act strategically." Stoesz and Raber (1994) add that "the purpose of planning is not to decide what should be done in the future but to decide what should be done now to make desired things happen in an uncertain future."

While these descriptions are valid and helpful, boards and staffs need something more to grasp the concept and purpose of strategic planning. They need to know the specific reasons for undertaking strategic planning, and they need to have some sense of the *precautions*, the things to guard against.

The Whys

A number of concrete, precise reasons can be marshaled to justify the value of strategic planning.

Mission change. Probably the most compelling reason for undertaking strategic planning, and also the most difficult to deal with, is when the underlying mission of the organization, its basic purpose, is brought into question. Several years ago, for example, the March of Dimes, the promotional name for the former National Foundation for Infantile Paralysis, went through a complete transformation when the Salk vaccine virtually removed polio from the scene. It changed its mission, turning its attention in an altogether new direction, becoming the March of Dimes Birth Defects Foundation.

The Washington Post recently carried a front-page article reporting that at George Mason University in northern Virginia students, professors, and local officials have become increasingly divided about the school's mission (O'Harrow Jr. and Lipton, 1996). Should the university provide traditional training for undergraduates, or should it serve the fast-changing needs of high-technology businesses and residents in the region? Any such thought of changing the basic mission of an organization unquestionably calls for strategic planning.

Organizational uncertainties. Nonprofit organizations often have to deal with changing circumstances around them and make adjustments less traumatic than fundamental mission change. Although organizations' fundamental purposes may be clear, the environments in which they act—both external and internal—are ever changing, calling for modification in how organizations do things. The process of strategic planning allows the leaders of such organizations to speculate, to peer into the crystal ball, and to bring to the surface the uncertainties, thus making possible a more informed way of moving forward.

Decision making. Boards, their chief executives, and their staffs all need a comprehensive and understandable basis for day-to-day decision making. Decisions in governance and management are more reliable when made deliberately, with full examination of possible future consequences, within the framework of a set of determined priorities, and in accordance with the perspective of *all* of the organization's programs and levels of authority. Strategic planning can give decisions that underpinning.

Fund raising. Most nonprofit organizations need to attract contributed money; many are wholly dependent on donations. A successful fund raising program rests on both a realistic determination of *funding needs* and a persuasive statement of *why* people should contribute support. These essentials can emerge best, and perhaps only, from strategic planning. Especially for organizations that are embarking on a major capital campaign for bricks and mortar or endowments, strategic planning is requisite; comprehensive planning is one of the key marks of readiness to undertake the commitment that such campaigns require.

Resource allocation. Of course all organizations—nonprofit, for profit, and governmental—must husband their resources and be constantly vigilant in expending their income and assigning their personnel. Board members of nonprofit organizations, as trustees, have a fiduciary role in financial responsibility. The budgets approved by nonprofit boards are financial plans for the short run; strategic planning enables boards to enact sensible resource allocation over longer periods of several budget cycles.

Performance evaluation. Criteria against which to measure and evaluate how well an organization is doing are established through strategic planning. Szanton (1992) makes the point that "the most challenging questions the board can ask, and the most important questions for the board to answer, must . . . deal with ends, with what results are being achieved. . . . There is no way to tell whether an organization is achieving its purposes unless somewhere those purposes are clearly stated."

Organizational effectiveness. Nonprofit institutions function as a team: the board, the executive, and the staff. The process of strategic planning inevitably throws a spotlight on team effectiveness. Particularly revealing is the focus it puts on board leadership. Strategic planning will measure board commitment and fulfillment of its responsibilities, board support and oversight of staff, and any micromanagement or invasion of the staff's management prerogatives. It will pinpoint the need for change in board composition, organization, or procedures.

Beyond giving clear guidelines for future programs, strategic planning can do much to strengthen the organizational fabric; indeed, planning activity can actually become the adhesive in an emerging team effort. While all of the foregoing reasons for doing strategic planning may not apply to all nonprofits, every organization will find meaning in at least some of them. A self-assessment checklist may help the organization to evaluate how it stands relative to each of these aspects of planning and thus highlight the need to embark on strategic planning.

In sum, organizations that avoid strategic planning are likely to miss opportunities to respond to inevitable or desirable change; they risk what no nonprofit organization can afford: falling out of touch with those they seek to serve, with their supporters, and with the general public, to whom they are responsible.

Precautions

Some volunteer board members have an underlying reluctance to face change, or simply have difficulty accepting the role of planner.

Others are unwilling to make the commitment of time or expense that may be involved. Still others are fundamentally skeptical, doubting the value of what can be produced in the exercise of planning. Such resistance calls for a clear expression of the advantages of strategic planning and what is involved in the strategic planning process, but it also highlights the need for candor on the difficulties and hazards.

Without question, in some situations strategic planning should not be undertaken. For instance, times of crisis—such as a major financial crunch, the precipitous departure of the chief executive, or turmoil and conflict among board members or between the board and the staff—are not propitious for successful planning. No organization should undertake strategic planning without the uncompromised support of both the board's chair and the chief executive.

Thus successful planning has a lot to do with readiness. A board is not ready for strategic planning if it is distant from the organization's operations or is meeting infrequently—in a word, if it is not leading. A dysfunctional, noninvolved board may well find a candid, uncompromising self-assessment to be the more useful course to take in place of or preceding strategic planning.

A common but unfortunate mistake is to confuse strategic planning, an essentially internal matter, with strategies for an improved public image. If strategic plans focus on how well the mission and vision will appeal to outsiders, the planning document becomes a public relations statement. It won't do the job. A strategic plan and the process by which it is generated are private; they are for the board to use, with staff support, to determine the organization's future. Only after the plan is formulated should the public relations implications be explored.

A survey questionnaire, no matter how elaborate or professional, no matter how wide a canvass of constituencies, and no matter how useful for other purposes, will not by itself accomplish strategic planning purposes. Polls of members or constituencies can be highly valuable as input to the strategic planning process, offering helpful insights and bringing focus to discussions, but they miss the intrinsic value of interaction, of debate. Planning sessions will not only change people's views, they will also generate new outlooks. The late Secretary of State John Foster Dulles used to say that new ideas come only from the clash of ideas.

No strategic planning process will be exactly right for all nonprofit organizations; "one size fits all" does not apply. Nor is strategic planning going to produce a solution to all problems; expectations must be realistic. However, the fear of complexity should not deter planning efforts. Although writers on strategic planning may introduce complex schemes and devices for resolving differing views on organizational purpose and priorities, such schemes and devices need not dominate the process or be reasons for board members to resist involvement. Some common objections to strategic planning are reviewed in Resource A at the end of the book.

Change and Continuity

Because strategic planning is linked to change, it can threaten the timid. While change is of course at the heart of strategic planning, the essence of good planning lies in balancing change and continuity.

In addition to fearing complexity, board members or staff may be reluctant to engage in strategic planning because they fear or are at least resistant to change. This fear or resistance is rarely acknowledged; people will say they are willing to consider change when in fact deep down they are not, perhaps because they fear loss of control or are protecting what they are used to and enjoy. Thus the often-heard expression "If it ain't broke, why fix it?" may stand in the way of thoughtful planning. The implication is, "We're going along fine; why not wait until we *have to* do something different." Yet change, if needed, can be easier to accomplish, and much more sensible and reliable, if made deliberately in peaceful times rather than in the middle of crisis. Think of it as preventive medicine: you take steps when in good health, you don't wait for the heart attack to stimulate action.

Such resistance to change can be strongest in a founding executive or chair who can't let go. This resistance is known as "founderitis": a strong leader who still contributes significantly to the organization's effectiveness but dominates decisions and consciously or unconsciously doesn't want it otherwise. However, to make changes that are not needed can be as damaging as to fail to make changes when they are needed. A paraphrase of a time-honored prayer is quite fitting to the circumstances of strategic planning:

> God give me the willingness to accept the things that
>   need to change,
> The courage to hold onto the things that need not
>   change,
> And the wisdom to know the difference.

The Business Analogy

One other, frequently misunderstood aspect of strategic planning warrants discussion at the outset—namely, the value of for-profit business models to nonprofit organizations.

Strategic planning in nonprofit organizations originally took its cue from for-profit business, especially corporate planning patterns developed at the Harvard Business School. While some business planning practices, including the exercise known as SWOT (successes, weaknesses, opportunities, and threats) can be helpful to nonprofit organizations (see Chapter Eleven), there remain important differences that limit the value of business planning systems.

For-profit businesses exist to make money. While strongly influenced by many nonfinancial considerations—such as market share, environmental impact, and public image—they always use a profit margin, a quantifiable bottom line, to guide their course, pattern their planning, and judge their effectiveness. Nonprofit organizations, on the other hand, exist to provide a public service, to afford benefits for members, or to support other nonprofits engaged in public service. Although they must never discount the importance of responsible financial management, nonprofit organizations, in determining programs to undertake and in evaluating their effectiveness, depend inescapably on *subjective* judgments, on balancing imprecise benefits against precise costs.

Business people active in philanthropy are instinctively inclined to seek to apply business planning procedures to their nonprofit affiliations. In some areas, such as financial management, this approach can be helpful, but not if financial considerations so dominate planning and operations that they override the underlying purposes of the organization.

While nonprofit organizations must always be financially responsible, and while many of their programs may have aspects that have useful numerical measures, they have to plan, and the effectiveness of much of what they do must be judged, on the basis of essentially nonfinancial, nonquantifiable, highly varied, and subjective criteria. It helps to start by examining the organization's mission and seeking out ways and criteria against which to measure success without relying on numbers.

Quantification may help, but in the end one doesn't judge the performance of a school or university by the number of students—though the best institutions will attract the most students—or even by their numerical grades but rather by whether their graduates are educated. How do you measure that? Organizations that care for the homeless are not judged by how many people they serve but by the quality of care they provide and the benefits that accrue to the community. Hospitals are a clear example: though they are overwhelmingly dependent on revenue earnings, including government reimbursements, and therefore have a bottom line they must observe, they exist to provide health care and in the final analysis are to be judged above all on that purpose.

A balance therefore needs to be struck: business models can be followed where they can be helpful, but throughout the organizational and procedural planning processes, nonprofit organizations must guard against expecting such models to be just the same as those for business.

2

The Board's Responsibility
for Strategic Planning

In nonprofit organizations it is the board's job to see that planning takes place and that it is done well. Because the board is ultimately responsible for the welfare and effectiveness of the whole organization, it is answerable for what the organization does and for how it does it. Accordingly, a board must not only assure that planning takes place and oversee the process, it must actively participate in the process.

This categorical view of the board's responsibility for planning is not shared by everyone. People in the for-profit business world, for example, often hold that the development of an organization's plans for the future should be the responsibility of those charged with implementing those plans—that is, the executive and the staff—and that the board's function should be to approve the plans and oversee their implementation. The rationale for this view is that because the board has to be in a position to question and to consider alternatives, it should not formulate the strategic plans itself, and it should not be committed to any single course.

Such an interpretation may be appropriate for a for-profit business, but it is probably not appropriate for a nonprofit organization. Because the board of a nonprofit organization is accountable for the organization's usefulness and effectiveness, for its present and its future, it must not only ensure that planning takes place, approve the product of planning—the strategic and operational plans—and ensure that implementation takes place, but it must also be an active participant in the planning process.

This view of the board's responsibility is emphasized by schools consultant James Wickenden (1995): "The best boards are constructive agents for change. They anticipate future demands and require the school's employees to meet them. They ask hard questions; they challenge the status quo. They set broad policies to accomplish the stated mission and then demand evidence that the polices are being followed."

Strategic planning is not easy; boards need to face up to the challenge. There will be boards that will want to turn over planning to a committee, to the staff, or to an outside consultant, because they believe that the board is fulfilling its responsibilities by reviewing and approving the product of planning. Rarely does one of these approaches work. A strategic plan prepared by others will not be the board's plan, and probably won't come near to fulfilling what the organization needs and has a right to expect from its leadership.

Because of the board's direct responsibility to lead the organization, it should either participate in the actual planning itself or it should certainly direct the manner in which the planning takes place. Indeed, to be successful a strategic planning effort requires the enthusiastic support of the board and the participation of at least its leaders.

The manner in which the board fulfills its role in strategic planning is in many ways quite different from how it handles its other responsibilities. While in most of what boards do they look to committees to delve into subjects and prepare recommendations, in strategic planning whole boards need to take an active part at each stage and be committed to its outcome. It is nevertheless altogether appropriate and advantageous for boards to appoint a standing or ad hoc committee—a *steering committee*—to make plans for planning. Such a committee will have the board's mandate to make recommendations on *when* and *how* planning should take place. Unlike other board committees, a steering committee will not deal with the substance of its charge, that is, the actual planning; instead it will focus the board's attention and make recommendations on each aspect of the planning process's organization and procedures.

Boards will want to ensure that a broad perspective is taken in the planning. Each board member brings to the process a different background as well as different skills and interests, as do the staff, supporters, volunteers, and constituents. It is essential that full consideration be given to all participants. For each organization, arrangements for strategic planning will vary in the relative degrees of involvement and impact of the board as a whole, the board committees, the executive and staff, the constituents, and the consultants. But the board holds overall responsibility for how planning is done and for the outcome.

To place the responsibility for strategic planning on the board is by no means to exclude the executive and key staff members. Quite to the contrary, the executive often plays a pivotal role in the process by recognizing the need for strategic planning, working with the board chair to make sure that planning happens, making sure that the planning team has adequate information, and ultimately implementing the plan.

The executive and senior staff should meet with and be helpful to the planning team, but their role in the meetings is sensitive and limited. Although they participate in the discussions, and certainly supply information, it is easy for them to dominate the discussions, and it is too easy for the board to let them. The responsibility for the outcomes, the plans for the future of the organization, lie with the board. The executive and staff are the servants of the board in carrying out what the board determines the organization will be and do.

3

Examples of Strategic Planning
from the Board Perspective

Some organizations routinely undertake strategic planning while others are pressed either by events around them or by conditions within to seek organizational or program adjustments. It is instructive to see examples of how organizations in various fields—health care, education, culture, religion—have approached strategic planning.

Fountain Valley School

The Fountain Valley School in Colorado Springs, an independent coeducational boarding and day school, has accepted strategic planning as a regular part of the discipline of management. The board had undertaken a full strategic planning effort six years earlier. The school's current exercise was triggered by a periodic reaccreditation review that called for penetrating self-assessments, by a pressing need for building and endowment capital funding, and by an underlying sense that the school somehow lacked a common sense of purpose and understanding about where the school was going. The board recognized that a formal process was a way of initiating discussion of agreements and disagreements that would help sort things out.

Hospice Care of D.C.

Although Hospice Care of D.C. is in a strong position as an independent home care hospice program, it faced the threat of uncertain

Medicare and Medicaid payments, of the potentially disturbing impacts of managed care on the hospice concept, and of potential competition from other hospices, both nonprofit and for-profit. The organization had the choice of either remaining independent or affiliating with either of two bigger organizations. The board decided to use strategic planning to help make the decision.

Piedmont Environmental Council

Having successfully defeated a threatened Disney theme park invasion, a battle to which it had devoted major effort and resources, and with sharply divided views on what should be its next course, the board of the Piedmont Environmental Council, located in Warrenton, Virginia, sought through strategic planning to clarify what role the council should play in the future of Virginia land preservation and environmental advocacy.

Pilgrim Society

Several factors led the leaders of the Pilgrim Society, of Plymouth, Massachusetts, to use strategic planning to clarify its mission and establish priorities: what some board members described as financial drift and dissipation, combined with a pressing need for both capital and operating funds; a lack of definition of mission, notably on the relative importance of the society's role as a museum, research institution, and historical society; a limited cadre of supporters, called members, who elect the trustees; and a relatively quiescent or dormant board of trustees.

Grand Canyon Association

The chair and executive director of the Grand Canyon Association, a cooperative support organization for the national park, were fearful that complacency would result from the financial success of its activities. They saw in strategic planning a way to invigorate the board in a reaffirmation of the association's mission while exploring the possibility of expansion of its role from providing services to the park, which were fully covered by earned revenues, to providing other services to be supported by contributions.

Alzheimer's Association

A concerted effort to develop a firmer partnership in fund raising between the national headquarters of the Alzheimer's Association, located in Chicago and responsible for the support of medical research and overall coordination, and its more than two hundred local chapters, which provide hands-on patient and family support, pointed to a need to deal with organizational adjustments to accommodate differing interests. The first step, a comprehensive board self-assessment carried out with the assistance of outside counsel, led to strategic planning, principally centered on governance matters rather than on the association's mission.

Grace Episcopal Church

Every few years, the parish of Grace Episcopal Church, located in Providence, Rhode Island, had undertaken planning in one form or another. The rector and the vestry leaders felt the need once again to rethink the parish's mission, to find a balance between its traditional affluent parish culture and the demands of a contemporary urban surrounding, and to come to grips with the generational changes occurring in the parish membership.

National Society of Fund Raising Executives, Washington, D.C., Chapter

The governance committee of the Washington, D.C., chapter of the National Society of Fund Raising Executives, a professional membership association, convinced the board that after four or five years the previous strategic plan was both out-of-date and no longer being followed. The committee recommended that through strategic planning the chapter's mission could be clarified, especially with respect to priorities in serving its members, while at the same time providing services to benefit the general public.

Gardner and Florence Call Cowles Foundation

The board of the Gardner and Florence Call Cowles Foundation, a fifty-year-old grant-making organization located in Des Moines, Iowa, consisted of six family members and two "outsiders." It chose to undertake strategic planning to resolve several issues affecting its future. For one, it needed to deal with the problem of board member succession. For another, on the question of grant-making guidelines, the foundation charter called for grants to be made in Iowa, principally for higher education, but only two family members, the president and another, still resided in Iowa. And, perhaps the most difficult matter, the board's current, quite deliberate policy calling for annual grants to be made in excess of the total return on its capital, which resulted in a predictable, continuing reduction of its asset base, highlighted the need at least to consider an orderly liquidation of the foundation. Strategic planning seemed to be the course to follow.

4

The Language of Planning

The late Jonathan Cook, founder of the Support Centers of America, pointed out that while in most professions—such as law, accounting, and medicine—definitions and usages of words tend to be clear and indisputable, in planning no agreement on terminology exists. Semantic differences can be a barrier to success in strategic planning. As one observer says, "Our bottomless capacity to feud over terminology is as old as the language itself" (O'Connor, 1995).

As they approach planning, board members and staff cannot avoid using the everyday words associated with any planning effort. They can, however, be helped by accepting a common set of terms, by being clear on definitions, and by using the words consistently as they proceed down the planning path.

In the battleground of disputed definitions, here is a set of terms and their meanings as they are used in this book. While arbitrary, they have been selected in the hope of achieving clarity.

Strategic Planning and Long-Range Planning

The terms *strategic planning* and *long-range planning* are used interchangeably. It is possible to develop fine distinctions between them—matters of time frame or methodology—but the exercise is hardly worth the effort.

Mission, Values, and Vision

In planning, the words *mission*, *values*, and *vision* are fundamental to the process. They therefore are discussed extensively in the chapters that follow. In briefest terms, however, the following definitions can be applied:

> *Mission:* an affirmation of the organization's purpose; why it exists.

> *Values:* a most elusive word, values are not *what* an organization does or *why* it does what it does, but rather the principles that underlie and guide *how* it goes about fulfilling its mission.

> *Mission statement:* sometimes the mission statement consists of a brief paragraph in a brochure explaining what an organization does; in this book, it is a more comprehensive affirmation of an organization's purpose and values.

> *Vision:* an expression of what an organization wants to be and do in the coming years. It is in fact the presumed principal outcome of the planning process.

Ends and Means

The notion of ends and means is a basic underlying and guiding concept that, as some authors, notably Cook (1987) and Carver (1990), have demonstrated, has a fundamental impact on all aspects of strategic planning. If organizations in their planning distinguish the *ends*, the desired outcomes, from the *means*, the methods of achieving those ends, they go a long way toward thinking clearly and arriving at useful planning outcomes.

Although the distinction between ends and means cannot be absolute, boards in their governance role are essentially concerned with ends while the executive and staff who manage the organization are responsible for means. Of course boards must also deal with means and staffs must deal with ends, but the board's principal function is to look toward purposes and results, and the staff's role is largely to deal with the means of fulfilling those ends.

Note the following examples that illustrate the difficulties in distinguishing between ends and means:

- *Educating the public* about an organization's mission and activities may be thought of as an end when in actuality it is a means of fulfilling the mission.

- No matter how critical it is to the organization, *organizing and strengthening volunteers* is a means of implementing the organization's programs, not the purpose or end of those programs.

- *Professional credentials and accreditation*, a focus of many medical and educational institutions and associations, are not ends but means of raising and maintaining performance standards for the whole profession.

- *Technological proficiency*, an undeniably desirable attribute for any nonprofit organization, helps to achieve ends but is not an end in itself.

In strategic planning, specific programs are correctly seen as means of fulfilling an organization's mission, but at the next level, that is, in planning the programs, the purposes of a program become the end and the program activities become the means. Thus a mathematics program can be one means of achieving the end of a strong educational program, but in planning the mathematics program component, the end sought is proficiency in teaching mathematics, and the several math courses are the means. Constant vigilance in distinguishing what are ends and what are means will enhance the strategic planning effort.

Objectives and Goals

Although it is too extreme to suggest that the words *objective* and *goal* should be banned altogether from planning, their use should be carefully guarded. For some people, objectives and goals are synonymous. Others use one of these words to refer to broadly stated purposes—such as an "outcome statement" to guide programs and management functions—while using the other to denote a more narrowly stated purpose—such as a precise, time-phased, measurable result. But there is disagreement about which term to apply to which purpose. Are goals broader, or are objectives?

It is particularly troublesome that objectives and goals can refer to either the *ends* or the *means*, or to both, and thereby confuse a valuable planning distinction. Of course it is acceptable to use the terms *objectives* and *goals* according to their common, generic meaning, to refer to some desired achievement, but it is best to avoid using these terms to refer to the specific outcomes of strategic planning.

Strategies and Tactics

While it is generally accepted that tactics are the methods or actions used to carry out strategies, either word or both words can refer to both *ends* and *means*. Although the adjective *strategic* avoids this ambiguity—any forward, comprehensive thinking can be described as strategic—the nouns *strategies* and *tactics* introduce confusion: "Our strategy is to provide the most effective health care"; "We must devise strategies to fulfill our purpose"; "The organization's tactics call for these activities." Be wary.

Policy

A dangerously abstract word, *policy* can refer to any one of a number of elements that a careful planning process needs to keep distinct: guiding principles, plans, courses of action, procedures, and ends and means. Because *policy* is such an elusive term, the claim that policy is for the board and implementation of policy is for the staff was long ago abandoned as a useful concept for organizations to employ.

Stakeholders and Constituencies

These two words are virtually interchangeable. They embrace all groups or individuals who are affected by or who might in any way influence an organization. It is awkward but often necessary to group into one aggregate all disparate peoples or segments of the community, in spite of their highly varied relationships to an organization: patients, clients, students, customers, contributors, grant makers, vendors, contractors, government agencies, financial institutions, critics, competitors, and associated organizations—all of whom can be said to be stakeholders or constituencies. Boards and staffs must respond in different ways to each individual or group.

In a fiduciary sense, leaders answer to the *general public* for the performance of their nonprofit organizations. But the general public is too inclusive to be considered a constituency or a stakeholder. On balance, the term *constituency* is preferred and is used in this book when referring to the several components of the community that are influenced by, or that themselves influence, an organization.

Tread the line carefully: be as precise as possible when using terms, but don't let semantic disputes bog down the planning discussions.

Part II

Preparing for Strategic Planning

There are two dimensions to the process of strategic planning: *preparing* for the planning—organizing and selecting the procedures, identifying the steps to be taken, and designing the process—and *conducting* the planning itself—the content, logic, form, and substance of the discussion that needs to take place in planning strategically. The chapters in Part Two explore the first dimension; the chapters in Part Three explore the second.

Success in strategic planning depends on the preparation, on the organizational and procedural steps adopted. These aspects of planning need to be carefully thought through, deliberately pursued, and explicitly set out for the participants. Chapter Five explains how to do this—to plan for planning. Two particular aspects of organization and procedures that can make or break strategic planning deserve separate treatment: the *design of planning meetings*, including off-site retreats, the subject of Chapter Six; and the *leadership of discussions*, including the use of outside professional consultants (often referred to as *facilitators*), reviewed in Chapter Seven. Chapter Eight offers examples of how several organizations have dealt with preparation for strategic planning, and Chapter Nine outlines action steps for dealing with the preparational aspects of planning.

Plans for Planning

Once the first essential step in moving down the strategic planning path has been made unequivocally clear—that the *responsibility* for planning is the board's—then it is possible to examine how the board fulfills that responsibility: by determining when to proceed with strategic planning—the *timing*; by determining who the *participants* in planning will be, including the roles of the *executive and staff*; by obtaining the views of the *constituency*; by assembling the *materials* to be used by the planners; by distributing a *planning team questionnaire*; and by *drafting reports*. These elements of planning will be examined in this chapter. Two other major elements of the board's responsibility for planning—determining the kinds of *meetings* to be held, including whether to meet off-site in retreats, and who will be responsible for *discussion leadership*, including the role of consultants—are taken up in subsequent chapters.

Timing

How often and how thoroughly planning is undertaken depends much on the determination of the organization's leaders—how convinced they are of the importance of strategic thinking—and on the board's willingness to set aside the time for planning. Some organizations go through a thorough strategic planning cycle every five or six years. They find that planning helps to keep the board and staff thinking strategically and prevents them from becoming absorbed in day-to-day operations. It also helps them to examine how their programs fit into the organization's future outlook. Other organizations, especially large ones whose planning represents a heavy and time-consuming load, expect to do major planning every ten or so years—a dangerously long time to put off such an important part of governance. Still other organizations undertake planning only when circumstances indicate the need. And some simply don't plan in any formal way.

Timing can also be related to circumstances—either inside the organization or in the external community—that may trigger a need for planning. Thus the departure of an executive officer, the pressure to mount new programs, or an acute budget squeeze can stimulate the strategic planning process. Alternatively, new competitive pressures in the external environment, impending loss or gain of major financial support, or opportunities to collaborate with similar organizations can offer reasons for self-examination through strategic planning. Acceptance of a need to make fundamental revisions in the mission is reason alone for mounting a strategic planning effort.

Just as organizations can undertake strategic planning either too frequently or not frequently enough, so the planning process can absorb too much board and staff time or be treated too lightly and not command enough attention. The planning *process* can overwhelm the *product*. No rules or guidelines exist for deciding how much time is needed. Board leaders and executives are called upon to recognize the demands of planning and to act deliberately, to lead. In doing so, the board can turn to its steering committee to keep watch, to recommend when external or internal conditions point to a propitious time for planning.

The question of how much time to spend on planning, how long the process should take, calls for a different array of decisions. Large, integrated national organizations, or major educational institutions, may need as long as two years, with many meetings to complete the process, whereas smaller, less complex local organizations can handle their planning adequately in a year's time or less. Especially if the mission is in question, a lot of time may be needed. *Be careful:* organizations tend to underestimate the time required to do thorough, comprehensive strategic planning.

The Participants

One of the first matters that the steering committee will need to address is who should actually do the planning—that is, who the participants should be. The presumption is that because of the board's overall responsibility for the organization, the board as a whole—and certainly as many of its members as possible—should participate in the actual planning effort. When a board is the appropriate size and has the will to devote the time to undertake the planning, the organization gains immeasurably from the commitment of its leaders. The board may be too big, however, to undertake the actual planning, or it may not be able to assemble all of its members for a sufficient time commitment. So the planning team— those who will actually do the strategic planning—may need to include more than board members. In such cases, the board then selects the other team members, often based on the advice of the steering committee. Key board leaders who command the respect of the whole organization should be on the team; so should the executive, as well as a few leading members of the staff.

The optimum size of the planning team will vary for each institution. For some organizations, a planning team of no more than ten may have the breadth of understanding of all the elements of the organization's activities to be fully effective, and the planning task may be limited. More likely, a planning team of twenty or even thirty will be effective. The risk of being unwieldy increases with the team's size, however.

When the full board does not itself do the planning, the advantage of a carefully selected planning team is that it can meet more frequently than the day or two that would normally be the limit you could expect for full board involvement. A balance needs to be struck between achieving wide participation and having flexibility in meeting schedules.

Constituency Views

A major consideration in strategic planning is the role of constituent groups in the process. Often if you look outside the organization you can find those who know it well and can offer to strategic planning a needed diversity of views. The steering committee and the board must forthrightly address the question of constituency input.

Nonprofit organizations all have constituencies; some have many, some only few; some constituencies may be important, some less so. Educational institutions have faculty, students, parents, and alumni—all intimately concerned with the future of the institution. Health care organizations have doctors, nurses, staffs, patients, and patients' families, each with an outlook that should not be overlooked. Cultural organizations—museums, theaters, and choral and dance groups—have audiences, artists, and beneficiaries who need to be considered. And all of these organizations have supporters. All have groups inside and outside of the organization that have a concern for and interest in the organization and that in one way or another need to be considered in the planning process.

Frequently, representatives of at least some constituency groups deserve to be members of the planning team and can be accommodated without disturbing the balance of interests in the planning sessions. Alternatively, constituency views can be obtained in other ways: by written *surveys*, by *interview programs*, or by *focus group meetings*.

The simplest way of tapping constituency views is by conducting written *surveys*. Straightforward answers to specific questions related to program performance, leadership, competition, public image, fund raising, or other subjects important to planning can be sought and tabulated for planning team use.

An *interview program* is usually more productive than written surveys but more difficult to mount. To be the most useful, interviews take time, preferably involve board members, and require systematic tabulation—not a trivial undertaking if representatives of many constituencies are asked to give thoughtful responses to sensitive questions.

Focus group meetings involve pulling together members of different constituencies, or groups of constituencies, in separate meetings where the collective opinions and recommendations of the constituency can be raised and discussed. Such meetings are especially valuable because they allow for exchanges of views within each constituency group. Focus groups have to be carefully managed, however, and can occupy the time and efforts of many people.

No matter how the views of key constituencies are collected and reported, they are an important element of strategic planning in nonprofit organizations.

Materials

To ensure successful planning deliberations, the steering committee, supported by staff, should deliberately determine what information materials, in addition to constituency views, will be assembled. When the board or planning team sits down to plan, its members will need to have digested information concerning the institution's history, programs, finances, fund raising efforts, and especially previous strategic plans. Such facts and reports can be assembled by the staff and made available in advance; the planning sessions should not be encumbered with the need to brief participants on background information.

Preparatory materials should include a draft of a *mission statement* or an existing one. A central task of the planning team will be to concentrate on the mission and on any modification it arrives at as a result of the planning discussions. Because the team will need to start with an initial version of the mission statement, the steering committee should be sure to have one available. The steering committee should not itself undertake significant revisions; that job is for the planning team.

Too many advance information materials can be overwhelming; they can be a wasteful diversion from the central task of the planning team. The team will be concentrating on evaluations, assessments, and projections, which can only arise in the planning sessions, not in the marshaling of facts and reports.

Planning Team Questionnaire

The board or planning team members will be better prepared for planning sessions, will have their thoughts focused, if they too have responded to a brief questionnaire (not to be confused with constituency surveys) in anticipation of the planning sessions. The chief value of such a questionnaire does not come from its tabulated results; rather, the value lies in the focusing of attention and in the thoughts stimulated in the planning team members as they answer the questions. Indeed, little value is gained from tabulated answers to such questionnaires, especially compared to the information gleaned in that manner from constituents; but participants will come to planning meetings better prepared to grapple with difficult concepts if they have spent some time finding out what they think by responding to the questionnaire.

The questionnaire should not be burdensome; rather, it can be interesting, as the following sample questions demonstrate:

- What has been your greatest satisfaction as a board member?

- What do you see as the greatest strength [success] of the organization?

- What concerns you as the organization's most trouble-some weakness [failure]?

- How would you rate the following issues in terms of their current importance to the organization?

- What subjects would you wish to be sure are raised at the planning sessions?

Report Drafting

The results of planning sessions need to be captured; at the least, draft reports should be put forward that reflect the discussions that take place. Transcripts of sessions may help those who prepare the notes, but they are not helpful as reports of the discussions. The object of such reports is to capture the essence, the substance, the consensus—not word-for-word what was said. It is well to plan ahead for whether such reportorial duties will be assigned to the staff or to designated board or planning team members.

6

Effective Planning Meetings and Retreats

The discussions held at strategic planning meetings are altogether different from the discussions that take place at usual business meetings. Planning participants must come at familiar subjects from wholly different angles. They are to be shaken into exploring unfamiliar concepts, facing the environment around them and the resulting challenges as if they had not been there before. The planning meeting is a process of coming to grips with an unfamiliar and perhaps unwelcome reality. Routine approaches must be abandoned.

Strategic planning is a serious, comprehensive activity; it cannot be treated lightly or superficially or anecdotally. If it is to succeed, planning must not be treated as ordinary board business.

Accordingly, strategic planning is most effectively carried out in special meetings—if possible, day-long and preferably in a retreat setting, that is, off-site—when they can be arranged. If board members can be persuaded to devote the time, and the organization can afford any extra expense that may be incurred, holding planning sessions away from office routines, preferably in pleasant surroundings, will usually be conducive to constructive discussions.

Retreats have an added advantage: they make for team building; they offer matchless opportunity to strengthen mutual confidence, trust, and respect among the members and between the board and staff.

The alternative to retreats—holding planning sessions in the usual board rooms and for less than a full day—is rarely adequate, especially if strategic planning is treated as simply an agenda item added to other business. Although greater attendance can be achieved in-house, getting through the complexities of planning discussions will be unlikely. The subject matter can really be tackled only in extended sessions of more than three or four hours. And concentration on the single topic of planning is essential.

The board decides where and when meetings should be held on the advice of the steering committee. Even a one-day or weekend meeting in a retreat setting may not be sufficient to cover the planning agenda. Two or three days can be devoted to planning if participants are willing to give the time, or if the organization is faced with such a crisis that its survival depends on a comprehensive restructuring or redirecting of its mission. Alternatively, two or three planning sessions can be scheduled over a longer period of time, stretching out the planning process.

An evening get-together preceding a special planning meeting or retreat can be a valuable part of the scenario. A reception, a dinner, or an after-dinner coffee makes for an informal, congenial setting in which to introduce the planning subject matter and prepare the participants for the following day's procedures. Such a gathering has advantages for boards whose members are not altogether familiar with each other or who have not previously been through the planning process.

Another advantage of the retreat format is the avoidance of pressure. Strategic planning cannot be rushed. On the other hand, you can't dillydally and expect to reach productive conclusions. Discussions must be outcome directed; discipline is essential.

Whether specially arranged at a usual place or off-site in a retreat setting, successful planning sessions depend on careful preparation—a casual approach is not appropriate. The importance of discussion leadership is described in Chapter Seven. In addition, careful arrangements (beyond the substantive matters described in

Chapter Five), the commitment of board members, and a truly open mind on the part of all participants are requisite to success.

The *arrangements* for planning sessions, the logistics—such as the time, the place, the meals, and the relaxation—are all important. People are most productive when physically and emotionally comfortable. Concentration on the subject can be maintained, interruptions and outside calls can be limited, and an orderly course of discussion through a logical progression can be sustained. Without this care, the planning effort can fail. It sometimes does.

The excitement of planning meetings, especially retreats, comes from exploring new ground, rethinking old ways, and strengthening what you do by reminding yourself why you do it. People who come into planning sessions with their own agenda are missing that great opportunity, and they may be keeping others from it. An open mind on the part of all participants is not always easy to achieve, but it can make the difference between success and failure.

Retreats may be trouble to arrange but they are usually remembered with great satisfaction.

7

Using Consultants and Facilitators

The question always arises of whether or not to bring in a consultant to help in the planning process. Consultants can advise on the preparation, the organization, and the procedures, and they can lead the discussions, be a facilitator in the planning sessions.

There are pros and cons.

Take the cons first:

- Present board leadership may be adequate to meet the need; they may be able to shift from a business meeting approach to leadership to strategic planning leadership. The board may feel, "We can get along without outside help."

- Some board members may be concerned that an outsider will not fully understand and will not be able to be brought adequately up to speed on the "special nature" of the organization—its programs, personalities, history, culture, finances, and so on.

- The board may simply feel, "We can't afford it."

There are several advantages, however, to using an outside consultant:

- As an adviser on the process, a consultant, who is used to the pitfalls of planning as evidenced in other organizations, can help with the various aspects of "planning for planning"—making the arrangements, creating the advance questionnaires, devising the scenario for a retreat, and assisting in actions that flow from the planning effort.

- To be successful, strategic planning meetings must be outcome driven; a consultant can guide discussions in the exacting planning process; a board chair or member, no matter how respected in board meetings, may have difficulty getting to closure on intensely debated subjects that arise in planning.

- Having an outsider lead the discussions will free the planning team's chairperson to enter into the fray, where his or her knowledge and experience may be especially valuable.

- As a meeting leader, an outside consultant not only can keep the discussion on track but also can raise the difficult questions, play devil's advocate, pressing the participants to get beneath the surface of complex and sensitive issues.

Consultants and facilitators are neutral; they will not take positions on substantive matters. They will be seen as objective, as detached from the issues under discussion. In the heat of argument, such detached discussion leadership may have special value.

Part of the process of strategic planning is to get the participants, especially the board, to buy into the plans, to feel ownership in whatever directions the planning takes. The successful consultant will abet this aspect of the process.

But do not expect the consultant to write the report on the planning session. The consultant can, however, work with the planning team, presumably supported by staff, to prepare the report, to ensure that it adequately reflects the discussions.

To provide a picture of the range of a consultant's assistance in strategic planning, a sample consulting plan is shown in Resource B.

The decision to retain counsel or to go it alone may hinge on whether the organization has had experience in planning and has board or staff people with the ability and time to lead the way through the process. Or it may depend on whether the issues before the organization are so critical or sensitive that outside expertise and objectivity would be helpful.

Some organizations cannot, or believe they cannot, afford an outside consultant. Consultant's fees will vary; you can expect to pay a consultant a thousand dollars or more for each day of a planning meeting, for whatever number of days are needed to prepare for the sessions, and for any earlier assistance in making plans for planning.

Once the board has decided to retain a planning consultant, it should get competitive bids. In addition to making the selection more informed, consultants' proposals help to focus attention on what is important and to clarify what to expect from them.

8

Examples of Boards Preparing
for Strategic Planning

It can be instructive to compare how organizations that determined to undertake strategic planning went about it. Who made the plans for planning? What was the composition of the planning team? Did the planning team meet in a retreat or in another type of meeting? Was an outside consultant retained? What information materials and what advance questionnaires were used?

The following reports discuss only the preparation, the organization, and the procedures employed by the organizations; the reports and outcomes are presented in Chapter Fourteen.

Piedmont Environmental Council

In undertaking strategic planning to determine what it wanted to do following its defeat of the Disney theme park, the executive committee of the Piedmont Environmental Council, with the approval of the board, made the plans for planning and at the outset retained a professional consultant to advise on preparations and to lead the strategic planning discussions. Ninety percent of the board and five or six senior staff, a total of approximately forty people, participated as members of the planning team. A full-day retreat, preceded by a congenial evening get-together that included preliminary discussion of the retreat agenda, was held at a conference center. A simple questionnaire and some information materials were distributed in advance of the retreat.

Fountain Valley School

Once the Fountain Valley School board determined it to be timely to proceed with another strategic planning exercise, the chairman of the board, the headmaster, and a board member who was experienced in strategic planning made the plans for planning. The board member, on a pro bono basis, also led all the planning discussions. Approximately three-quarters of the board, with eight senior administrative staff and six senior faculty, a total of thirty-three people, formed the planning team.

The first planning session, a full-day retreat, was held at a local hotel, followed by three two-hour sessions at successive quarterly board meetings; it thus took a year to complete the process. An exhaustive accreditation exercise that preceded the planning retreat produced useful materials and perspectives. These were supplemented by summary reports on key programs, prepared by the faculty and staff and distributed to the planning team members in advance.

Hospice Care of D.C.

The scope of the planning assignment of Hospice Care of D.C. was specific and limited to the question of merging or remaining independent. The board designated specific members to prepare recommendations on each of three alternative courses that could be followed: associate with a hospital group, associate with a nursing home, or continue as an independent organization. The board created a planning committee consisting of fourteen board members to preplan the planning process. That committee, augmented by three former board members and with the participation of the hospice chairperson and the executive director, made up the planning team. Hospice Care's vice chairperson was designated leader of the committee and led the planning team discussions. No consultant was used. At a day-long retreat held in the home of a board member, detailed proposals for each of the options, which had been distributed prior to the retreat, were discussed.

Pilgrim Society

In accepting the need for strategic planning to clarify its mission, the executive committee placed responsibility on a long-range planning committee chaired by the society's vice president and composed of eight board members and the executive director. The committee not only set the procedures, it also did the actual planning. Reports on selected critical issues were prepared by subcommittees. The committee convened a focus group with representatives of various agencies in Plymouth and sent out a questionnaire to the trustees to elicit their reflections on the society's activities and programs. The trustees, along with some staff members, met with the planning committee in a colloquium that served as a major fact-finding session for preparation of the report.

Grand Canyon Association

The chairman of the board and the executive director of the Grand Canyon Association did the preplanning for the association's strategic planning process when they wanted to forestall complacency in the overall financial well-being of the association. No advance fact-finding was undertaken and no materials were prepared. A brief questionnaire was sent out in advance of the retreat, along with some program materials to be discussed. A professional consultant was retained to lead the discussions. The planning team, consisting of eight members of the nine-member board and four or five staff members, met in an evening gathering and full-day retreat. The planning session was followed by a regular board meeting.

Alzheimer's Association

To put special attention on a stronger governance structure and enhance the partnership of headquarters and chapters, the association used a limited strategic planning procedure. An ad hoc governance work group composed of eight members of the board—half drawn from association chapters, half "public members"—along with the chief executive and vice chief and led by a public member, did the preplanning and served as the planning team. A consultant on board development participated but did not lead the discussions. The planning team met frequently: three times in conjunction with quarterly board meetings, three or four times in two-hour telephone conference calls, and once for a two-day retreat led by a meeting facilitator (not the consultant).

Grace Episcopal Church

Spurred on by an urge to rethink the parish mission, the church turned to strategic planning as it had from time to time in the past, retaining a professional consultant to advise on planning for the planning session. The planning team consisted of the twelve vestry members, five former members, four nonvestry chairs of committees, and the rector. They met in an evening gathering, followed by a day-long retreat led by the consultant. A questionnaire designed to focus the attention of planning team members on selected issues was distributed in advance of the session.

National Society of Fund Raising Executives, Washington, D.C., Chapter

When the need for a review of the mission was pressed upon the chapter by the governance committee, it was given the responsibility for the planning. Thus, the vice chair for governance and the committee of eight diversified chapter members did the preplanning and served as the chapter's planning team. The team met twice and generated its own materials. No consultant was involved.

Gardner and Florence Call Cowles Foundation

To look at board member succession and to review the foundations's grant-making guidelines, the foundation's two fourth-generation board members, joined by the outsider board member, who was experienced in foundation management, were asked by the board to be the planning team for preparing a strategic plan. Without consultant assistance, the team created its own plans for planning and met in planning sessions four times, twice in telephone conference calls.

Varying challenges and needs will govern the manner in which nonprofit organizations will engage in strategic planning. So also, the governance structure, the organizational tradition, and the sophistication of the board will be strongly influential on how they go about planning.

9

Action Steps
Preparing for Strategic Planning

In approaching strategic planning, the board must recognize that preparation is important. To go directly into the substance of plans can give rise to confusion and frustration. A number of specific steps are called for to prepare.

1. The board acknowledges the importance of and its responsibility for strategic planning.

2. Acting on its own or on the recommendation of a standing committee or the chief executive, the board decides to undertake strategic planning and appoints a steering committee to make the preparations, the plans for planning.

3. The steering committee recommends for board review the organization and procedures for carrying out the planning:

    a. *Participants:* the members of the team that will undertake the actual planning, including board leaders, if not the full board; the executive and senior staff members; and any representatives drawn from constituencies (beneficiaries, donors, or others important to the organization)

    b. *Consultants,* if any, and their role

    c. *Constituency views:* to be gathered from interview surveys, questionnaires, or focus group meetings

    d. *Materials*: to be assembled for planning team members, including a draft or existing mission statement.

4. The steering committee makes out the schedule and arrangements for planning meetings or retreats:

    a. Time, place, and schedule

    b. Leadership

    c. Composition of break-out groups (groups that deliberate on separate aspects of the planning and report to the plenary session)

    d. Reporters to draft the findings

5. The steering committee prepares a participants' questionnaire to focus their attention before the meeting.

6. The steering committee arranges a social meeting to help the planning team participants get acquainted before the meeting.

Having made the foregoing preparations, the board or the planning team the board appoints is ready to come to grips with the substance of planning, to conduct the planning itself.

Part III

Conducting Strategic Planning

The central purpose of strategic planning sessions, aside from stimulating the organization to think strategically, is to confirm or modify the organization's *mission*—its basic purpose and values—and to agree on a *vision* of what the organization wants to be and do in the coming years. The outcome of the planning sessions will form the basis of a formal *strategic plan*.

The logical progression of steps for achieving this outcome is by no means as simple as it may appear. It does not help, for instance, for an organization simply to postulate some alternative visions of the future and then to evaluate the relative desirability and effectiveness of each option, select one, and expect it to be a realistic outcome of planning. To arrive at a vision that can be the basis for a useful strategic plan requires a deliberate pattern of movement along a prescribed logical course.

By no means is there universal agreement on the best course to take to achieve a clear and useful vision. Wise and honest people disagree, sometimes forcefully, on the path to follow in strategic planning, especially in regard to such concepts as purposes, values, and vision. Using different vocabularies, experts describe a varied progression of logical steps to reach differently defined outcomes.

The time frame of strategic plans sometimes is, but need not be, an obstacle in the process. As long as the horizon of planning goes beyond the budget cycles of the next year or two, planning can proceed confidently. If need be, the number of "coming years"—three, five, or ten—can be specified to afford a planning perspective.

The following four-step logical process, elaborated on in the next few chapters, seeks to achieve simplicity and clarity in reaching a comprehensive yet practical outcome:

1. Be explicit about the current *mission*—the purpose and values—though it may be modified as a result of the planning process (Chapter Ten).

2. Explore the *environments* the organization faces, both *external*—the opportunities and threats—and *internal*—the strengths and weaknesses (Chapter Eleven).

3. Identify the *critical issues* on which the future of the organization most directly depends (Chapter Twelve).

4. Articulate the *vision;* confirm or modify the mission and create a concept of the ends to be sought in the coming years and the means to achieve those ends, particularly with respect to the critical issues (Chapter Thirteen).

Chapter Fourteen uses the examples introduced in Chapters Three and Eight to illustrate how several organizations have proceeded down this logical path to reach strategic planning outcomes. And Chapter Fifteen recommends action steps for conducting strategic planning.

10

Clarifying the Mission
Purpose and Values

I f the outcome of strategic planning is to confirm or modify the
organization's mission and to set out the vision of what the organization wants to be and do in the coming years, the process must
start with its current mission—its *purpose*, why it exists—and its
values—the principles that underlie how it fulfills its purpose. Purpose can be precise; values are imprecise but no less important.

Purpose

Nonprofit organizations tend to take their purposes for granted, to
assume that everyone knows and agrees on why the organization
exists. But differences soon emerge when members of a group seek
to define the purpose.

Cook (1987) defines purpose as follows: "Every nonprofit organization exists because of some condition ('focus problem') in the
environment which it seeks to change. . . . An organization's purpose follows from its choice of focus problem. Partial or total solution of that focus problem is its purpose—the ultimate result an
organization exists to achieve. . . . Once the focus problem is clear,
the purpose will follow readily from it." Thus all institutions have
focus problems. Museums, health care, educational, and public policy organizations all seek a change for the good, all strive to make
a difference. Their purposes are to do something about the change

they feel is needed, the improvement they see called for, the void they perceive needs to be filled.

A statement of purpose articulates these reasons for existence, defines the ends and lays out the means, the methods to be used to carry out the purpose. A useful statement of purpose will thus identify the following:

- The *problem or condition to be changed*—such as misuse of natural resources, birth defects, poverty, and lack of appreciation for the arts; the dimensions of the problem; and what happens if the problem is not dealt with

- The *beneficiaries of change*, such as youth, the earth, minorities, the disadvantaged, animals, government agencies, and so on

- The *nature of the change to be sought,* using words such as "to improve," "to preserve," "to prevent," "to heal," or "to conserve"

- The *means or methods of change*, such as training, advocacy, research, or direct service

Values

Values differ from purpose but they are very much a feature of the mission. Values are not what the organization does but the way it does it.

The word *values*, however, like the word *vision*, can be a source of confusion. As Eadie (1993) says, "Values are the most cherished beliefs and principles that guide the nonprofits planning and operations; they provide the ethical framework of rules that transcend mere policy." Values are not purposes—that is, ends; nor are they programs—that is, means. They are principles, intrinsic elements of what the organization is all about, and therefore part of its mission. Be prepared: it can be a major challenge to identify and clarify these underlying values, and to distinguish them from ends and means. Board members may resist discussing elusive values.

As a stimulant to thinking about values, but not to provide a model, Peter Relic, president of the National Association of Independent Schools, speaks of some of the beliefs and values he looks for in schools he visits (Relic, 1995):

- I look for children involved in their learning.

- I look for color and light and movement.

- I look for, I hope for, pervasiveness of the arts.

- I look for incredibly high standards and expectations and support for the academics.

- I look for math and science and a school that somehow looks like it's preparing children for the 21st century.

- I look for social studies that somehow seem to be preparing children for this global village that we live in already.

- I look for joy and silliness and curiosity and imagination.

- I look for uncertainty and risk-taking.

And so on. Such a list is a good way to approach the subject of values: What would an informed visitor look for?

Following are other examples that illustrate the values that guide organizations in seeking to fulfill their purposes.

The Pilgrim Society

For its fundamental values, the Pilgrim Society draws on principles set out by the American Association of Museums (1992):

1. The commitment to education as central to museums' public service must be clearly expressed in every museum's mission and pivotal to every museum's activities.

2. Museums must become more inclusive places that welcome diverse audiences, but first they should reflect our society's pluralism in every aspect of their operations and programs.

3. Dynamic, forceful leadership from individuals, institutions, and organizations within and outside . . . the museum community is the key to fulfilling the museum's potential for public service in the coming century.

The Grand Canyon Association

The Grand Canyon Association maintains that "every visitor must be given every opportunity to learn as much as they want to learn about the Grand Canyon and its resources—physical, scientific, cultural, aesthetic." That is a statement of value.

Hospice Care of D.C.

Hospice Care of D.C. has many underlying values but two stand out: (1) every person who chooses the hospice deserves a dignified death: comfortable, pain free, spiritually fulfilled, and if possible in a place of their choosing, such as at home; and (2) the hospice is a celebration of life.

Piedmont Environmental Council

The Piedmont Environmental Council lives by the conviction that Northern Virginia, as beautiful open space and as a historical region, deserves to be preserved as a national heritage.

Grace Episcopal Church

Grace Episcopal Church, like any religious institution, is guided by the principles of its faith, but with one special feature: unlike many churches, it holds the sacrament of communion to be a community, not simply a personal celebration.

Gardner and Florence Call Cowles Foundation

The Gardner and Florence Call Cowles Foundation looks for worthwhile projects that demonstrate leadership and innovation, and makes grants for ventures that would not happen if it were not for the foundation's support.

The National Society of Fund Raising Executives

The National Society of Fund Raising Executives (NSFRE) introduces its strategic plan (1993) with this statement that can be taken as an articulation of its underlying values: "Philanthropy—voluntary action for the common good—is a necessary element of civic betterment and those activities which meet societal needs. Fund raising is an essential discipline in the philanthropic process. . . . NSFRE members and affiliates enable people and organizations to better serve diverse communities and society as a whole."

Collins and Porras (1994) make an unusual suggestion that can apply as a value to almost any organization: "A drive for progress is never satisfied with the status quo even when the status quo is working. . . . Good enough . . . never is."

Mission Statement

The difficulty in drawing up a mission statement—a definition of purpose and values—is in making it broad enough to encompass all that an organization does yet keeping it narrow enough to give it focus, to differentiate it from other mission statements, to give it a sharpness that will be a realistic guide.

Hodgkin (1993) points out, "The process of mission definition is extraordinarily complex, often fuzzy, and generally philosophical, constituency-based, and value-oriented." And Drucker (1990) adds: "The best nonprofits devote a great deal of thought to defining their organization's mission. They avoid sweeping statements full of good intentions and focus, instead, on objectives that have clear-cut implications for the work their members perform—staff and volunteers both."

A key feature of a mission statement should be the answer to the simple question: What sets this organization apart from others? The answer may have to do with the organization's basic purpose—what it does that is different—or something in its values—how it goes about fulfilling its purpose—that makes the organization distinctive, but the mission statement should place this distinguishing feature front and center.

Shun the word *unique*. Every organization and program is unique, and none is. Using this word tells you nothing about the organization or the program.

Planning teams must have access to a current mission statement, either historical or newly drafted, to begin planning deliberations. A measure of agreement on purposes and values is essential before going on to the next steps in the planning process.

The initial mission statement can present a dilemma. It is all too easy to spend endless hours nitpicking the statement. Do not get too absorbed in this first step, because the mission—either reaffirmed or modified—is precisely what will emerge from the planning process. Let the discussion bring out areas of full agreement and points of possible controversy, and then get on with the planning process. Don't let the search for a fully agreed-upon, detailed current mission statement be an obstacle.

A start must be made; reviewing the initial mission statement is the best way to begin.

11

Exploring Internal and External Environments

If strategic planning is about the future of the organization, it surely follows that the conditions and forces that will have an impact on that future need to be explored. Planning efforts fail, or fall short in their strategic purpose, when discussions start with where an organization currently is and put attention only on how it can improve what it is now doing, rather than starting by looking ahead to what kind of environment, what conditions, can reasonably be expected, and then determining the kind of organization it will need to be to meet those conditions.

Future conditions are of two kinds: *external* conditions—things outside the organization that can have an important impact and that usually cannot be influenced; and *internal* conditions—things within the organization that probably can be changed.

In scanning both the external and internal environments, the planning team deals with three kinds of information on which to build its planning efforts:

- *Facts and figures:* hard data such as economic and demographic studies; the history of the organization; financial statements; program statistics; and professional analyses in the organization's field, such as the arts, health care, or education

- *Constituency views:* facts and opinions gleaned from meetings or surveys of interested groups, such as board committees, staff, volunteers, donors, clients, competitors, and beneficiaries

- The results of *brainstorming:* the planning team thinking together, speculating, and exchanging views

All three types of information are important. The facts and figures and the constituency views can be gathered and absorbed in advance; the brainstorming takes place during the planning sessions.

Put the emphasis on brainstorming. The tendency is strong to lean too heavily on facts and figures and thus to underestimate the value of group speculative thinking. Although planners must rely on reports, statistics, and authoritative analyses, and although they must certainly take into account the views of constituents, they can be overwhelmed by materials. Moreover, brainstorming has hidden values. When the planning team discusses at the outset possible future influences, it will not only promptly find itself thinking strategically, it will also turn up insights and evaluations not found in the facts and figures or in the views of constituents. Don't underestimate the planning team's capability in crystal ball gazing; weird and wonderful ideas spring out that can lead to thoughtful plans.

Planning teams use various methods for dealing with external and internal environments. Classically, the SWOT procedure—the successive examination of the strengths and weaknesses of the internal environment and of the opportunities and threats of the external environment—is called into play. Whether this formula is followed rigorously or loosely, it is better to consider the external before the internal; organizations have no trouble thinking about themselves, but they do have trouble looking outside.

Examining the External Environment

The organization's mission statement will have pointed out that the organization exists to fulfill a social need. In its assessment of the external environment, the planning team looks at the demographic, political, economic, regulatory, or other emerging forces or trends that the organization may have to face in meeting the social need, in fulfilling its mission.

When planning teams turn to examining the external environmental forces, the participants join in throwing out ideas, guesses, and speculations—some with merit, some extreme. All the possibilities can be recorded on flipchart sheets. The external forces discussed can vary from government actions to constituent needs, from competitive dangers to accreditation problems—all of them largely beyond the organization's control. The planning team identifies which among these forces are the opportunities and which are the threats, the barriers to overcome, and by means of discussion or even by voting on rank order, assigns each force a relative importance and urgency. The planning team thus ends up with something less than a precise forecast but considerably more than a blank picture of what the organization faces as it looks to the future. No definitive conclusion needs to be reached; the real gain comes from having the planning team think about the organization and its future in terms of these forces.

Examining the Internal Environment

Turning within the organization, speculative thinking can suggest an array of internal factors that in the coming years are likely to have an impact on the organization's ability to fulfill its stated mission. The suggested internal environmental factors can be arbitrarily categorized, similarly to the external factors, as strengths and weaknesses, and their relative importance can be evaluated.

In sorting out strengths and weaknesses, the possible impacts on the organization of the basic elements of management—*inputs, process,* and *outputs*—can be examined. Thus, with respect to *inputs,* the planning team can investigate, with its eye on the future, such matters as human resources, supplies, facilities, and funding. In regard to *process,* it can examine what attention needs to be given to organizational systems and functions, to programs and projects.

The last of these internal environmental factors, the *outputs,* or the performance, may be the most important and the most difficult. Candid evaluation of program performance stands out as a prime ingredient of successful strategic planning; future plans hinge directly on how well the organization is fulfilling its mission, and how well it can carry it out in the future.

Remember that the criteria for program evaluation are always unclear. Nonprofit organizations exist to provide a public service, a service to members, or a grant-making service. The effectiveness of their performance has to be evaluated against essentially nonfinancial, nonquantifiable, subjective judgments of success that vary for each field of endeavor. In education, for example, as noted earlier, success is not judged by the number of students enrolled in an institution but by whether the students are educated—criteria that are close to impossible to standardize. Other community service organizations that care are not judged by the number of people they serve but by the quality of care they provide, and who is to define that quality? Hospitals in particular, while dependent on revenue earnings, exist to provide health care and are to be judged on the quality of that care and not on the organization's financial acuity.

Because of the intrinsic importance of performance to planning, the planning team must come to grips, no matter how elusive the data may be, with the evaluation of how well the organization is performing and can perform. That is the output, an internal environmental element that cannot escape attention.

Crystal clarity and certainty will not emerge from environmental assessments. But the planning process will proceed on a sounder basis and with a realistic perspective because of the attention given to these external and internal forces.

12

Identifying the Critical Issues

At the center of strategic planning is the selection of *critical issues*. The planning team cannot cover every facet or make plans for every corner of the organization. It must home in on those issues that deserve full attention, those most central to the organization's future.

The focus must first be on *ends*—what does the organization want to achieve with reference to the selected critical issues? Ends, in Carver's terms, are "what human needs are satisfied, for whom, and at what cost" (1990). Once the ends are identified, the *means* can be explored—how to achieve the ends, or what programs or changes are necessary to attain the ends.

If strategic planning is about the vision of what the organization wants to be and do in the coming years, it must look to the areas that will be truly determinant in that vision, to determine the ends it seeks to attain in the coming years and to decide what it must do to reach those ends. In an important sense, strategic planning is the path from present ideas to new and different courses of action for the future. The ends and means in selected critical issues are the link in the process.

Critical or strategic issues are fundamental questions that go to the heart of the organization's mission and values. What are the key points that will determine the organization's ability to deal with the environment it must anticipate? With ends and means in mind, what changes in kinds or levels of services, what adjustments in constituency relations, promotion, organizational design, and finances will most directly affect the organization's performance in fulfilling its mission?

Selecting the critical issues to explore is a challenge to the planning team. It will need to be deliberate, to spend time on the selection process, paying attention to constituency views, to what issues staff, donors, beneficiaries, and clients see as critical; but in the end, the team itself will have to select what needs to be dealt with and what can be set aside. Seeking to embrace too many critical issues at once can threaten the process. Six or seven should be the maximum, but possibly as few as three or four would be better.

To assist in narrowing down the selection of key issues, a common practice is to have the planning team list all the possible issues, then to have each member separately select the top five or six issues in priority order, then to tabulate the votes. Inevitably, some planning team members will be concerned that an important issue did not make the grade and therefore is not included in the list of critical issues on which attention will be put.

The natural temptation to preselect the critical issues should be resisted. The planning team gains much in the process it goes through to arrive at its selection. The best critical issues on which to concentrate may not be the obvious ones. Schools, for instance, would need to guard against selecting a prosaic array that simply reflects their constituencies—students, faculty, parents, and alumni—or a functional breakdown, such as finances, physical plant, and governance. In doing so they could miss some crosscutting issues such as curriculum, extracurricular activities, student life, and community. In much the same way, a community service organization might usefully center its planning on such critical issues as its client composition—the kinds of people to be served, the organization's image, the promotion of its services, and its financial stability. Although the critical issues should be few in number, the selection must reflect the whole organization rather than be confined to administrative or specific program issues.

In the Amherst H. Wilder Foundation's *Strategic Planning Workbook*, author Barry (1996) suggests in a worksheet a sample array of critical issues:

1. Should our mission be broadened to include middle- and upper-income people?
2. If we serve a broader range or people, what image do we want to convey (with our name, facilities, and so on)?
3. How can we move toward financial independence—that is, less reliance on vulnerable federal dollars?
4. How can we maintain a skilled, stable, professional staff?
5. What kind of facilities will be needed? Where should they be located?
6. What kind of board will be needed in the future? And how can we make the transition?

The planning team must center its deliberations on the ends it wants to achieve, and it must not be diverted to means until it has identified the ends. Although matters of organizational structure, board development, staff organization, or board-staff relations may properly be identified as important and needing attention, they are in fact means, not ends; "remedies" in these matters may be better addressed separately by the board in a self-assessment exercise, rather than as part of strategic planning.

At this point in the strategic planning process the planning team must come to grips with what it collectively believes should be done about each of the selected critical issues. What changes should be made? What are the ends it wants to seek, and what are the means needed to accomplish those ends?

The usual procedure is to divide the planning team into "break-out" groups that meet separately. Each break-out group concentrates on a single issue and, mindful of the external and internal environments and of the views of constituents, comes up with considered views and specific recommendations on the particular issue.

Detail is not important. However, aside from constant attention to ends and means, two things count heavily: clarity and realism. An unclear, vague, generalized suggestion for change is not helpful; break-out group recommendations must be specific and unequivocal. Suggested new directions or changes in ends or means must fully recognize the barriers to achievement, the difficulties that will stand in the way of moving in a chosen direction. A recommendation for a different course, briefly and clearly stated, that reflects a clear understanding of the demands it poses is the mark of successful planning.

The break-out groups come together to report on their progress. Then the planning team goes on to complete its part in the planning process.

13

Articulating a Vision

Although the ultimate products of strategic planning are the formal strategic and operational plans, the principal substantive purpose of the planning exercise will be achieved in the report of the planning team. Leaders will have become engaged in thinking strategically. Through the planning sessions, the team will have created a design, the conceptual basis for the operation of the organization for the coming years.

The report of the planning team is in fact the articulation of the vision. It will directly confirm the mission or clearly define its modification. It will, in Greene's words, be a "description of your organization's preferred future state," describing "the activities, structure, scale and resources needed for your organization to have a significant impact on the achievement of its purpose" (1988).

In its final plenary session, the planning team should have before it the recommendations of the several break-out groups proposing where the organization should go on each of the selected critical issues. Or if break-out groups were not used, the planning team itself, possibly in several meetings, may take up each critical issue and reach conclusions on the ends the organization should seek and the means it should use to achieve those ends. In either case, an agreement is reached in the planning sessions that can be the basis of a report that sets out the way the organization will look in the years ahead. The report can be drafted following the sessions by those appointed to do the job.

The report need not be long. It will reaffirm the mission, including both its purposes and its values, incorporating any changes that emerged from the planning sessions. It can mention the external and internal environments that underlie the report's conclusions. Its principal message, however, should be in its conclusions—the changes, the directions, the priorities that the planning team recommends for the years ahead.

Think of the various directions, all of them controversial, that might be appropriately suggested in a report of the planning team:

- No change whatsoever

- To grow; to add programs

- To downsize; to quit programs

- To go out of business altogether

- To merge with another organization

- To narrow the specialization

- To become entrepreneurial

- To professionalize

- To deprofessionalize

- To change the client/beneficiary focus

- To shift sources of support

Each course has its risks, its barriers to overcome. Each calls for internal, possibly major adjustments. Indeed, some of the indicated changes may be entirely internal: a new governance structure, staff realignment, changes in volunteers, resource reallocation, and changes in facilities, performance criteria, and ethical standards.

Priorities will probably be a central focus of the report. Drucker (1990) emphasizes the difficulties in dealing with priorities because the process "always involves abandoning things that look attractive, or giving up programs that people both inside and outside the organization are strongly pushing for. . . . This may be the ultimate test of leadership: the ability to think through the priority decision and to make it stick."

Thus the report of the planning sessions is an unambiguous declaration of what the organization wants to be and do—its vision. The report will be better for being short and lucid—and it should definitely not be a boilerplate. It should avoid such meaningless words as "excellence" and "unique." It should be realistic in the sense that it should envision pragmatically the obstacles to be overcome. It should be drawn up with the deliberate intention of being the conceptual basis for the more comprehensive, more formal strategic plan.

Examples of
Strategic Planning Outcomes

Just as planning activities will vary for organizations of different kinds and sizes, so it can be expected that the level of success, the degree of fulfillment, will be different in each case of strategic planning. Sometimes, for any number of reasons, little is achieved in a strategic planning exercise. However, through effective strategic planning both mature and young struggling institutions can make major changes in mission, priorities, and organization. Some organizations, especially those not accustomed to planning, may attain an important measure of success in their first planning effort if only by achieving a better understanding of their own purposes, values, and activities; increasing board involvement; or simply determining to go on to the next steps in planning.

No markers exist for scoring success in strategic planning. Outcomes can be examined in terms of how directly the mission and vision were addressed, and in terms of the comprehensiveness, clarity, and overall value of the recommendations that emerged from the process. On the other hand, planning that had limited purposes must be judged differently, in relation to the purpose.

Piedmont Environmental Council

After the full board and senior staff of the Piedmont Environmental Center met in a day-long retreat setting to address its post Disney theme park future, a volunteer board member working with the chairman and the executive committee prepared a ten-page report. The report underwent several drafts, and was formally approved by the board.

The planning effort had several positive results: a fully acceptable statement of the council's vision, including a reaffirmation of its mission; a reshaping and retargeting of its public message; a strengthening of its programmatic efforts at the local level; and a revisioning of the organization and procedures of the board itself.

The planning team's report set out the lines for a formal strategic plan and separate operational plans for the programs, appropriately timed for the installation of a new chair and new executive. The strategic planning process was a success along classic lines.

Fountain Valley School

A wide area of agreement emerged from the Fountain Valley School's year-long process in which the planning team of board, faculty, and staff met on a retreat, followed by several special board sessions. An eight-page report drafted by a staff member and reviewed by the headmaster and retreat leader was approved by the board. The report was made into a strategic plan that set out a revised mission statement and established five-year goals for each of the following issues: admissions, academic/curriculum program, alumni/development, faculty, finance, and student life/residential. Operational plans were then prepared by staff and reviewed by board committees. These plans were available for periodic reference by the committees or the full board; they served as a road map for guiding school programs and budgeting.

This strategic planning example followed classic lines in its time span, leadership, comprehensiveness, and outcomes, producing useable documentation to guide programs in the coming years and, not insignificantly, establishing realistic funding needs and forming the basis for a case for strong fund raising support.

Hospice of D.C.

Because the mandate to the Hospice of D.C.'s planning team had been limited to a single and controversial issue, the process differed significantly from the normal pattern of strategic planning. Though the future of the organization was at stake, the purpose was in fact issue resolution rather than strategic planning.

Though its mandate was limited and specific—to recommend whether to remain independent or merge with one of two possible related organizations—the planning team, in its day-long retreat, was unable to come to agreement. The problem was returned to the board, which after two special meetings made the decision to merge with one of the organizations, subject to negotiating an acceptable merger arrangement.

Though unsuccessful in its outcome, the planning exercise did have benefits as the result of the preparations that went into it and the depth of understanding its leaders attained in the sessions; the ultimate decision taken by the board was thus more informed and measured.

Pilgrim Society

The Pilgrim Society's long-range planning committee drew up a report of thirty pages that contained an evaluation of the society's museum and educational mission and the recommendations of the committee. A separate appendix contained the texts of all sub-committee reports and other documentation.

The report endorsed a 1951 statement of the goals and purposes of the society, with two exceptions, one relating to priorities, the other to land holdings; at the same time it restated the goals in a different form. The report then set out a series of near-term and long-term recommendations, recognizing that the latter would "require considerable time and effort and may require substantial restructuring of programs, services and methods of operation." The committee made recommendations on the following subjects:

1. Exhibits, including climate control and security
2. Manuscripts, library, and genealogy
3. Education, lectures, and publications
4. Property and development options
5. Finances and development
6. Governance and administration
7. Membership
8. Accessory issues, including other historical organizations, local perceptions, celebration ceremonies, historic preservation, and the fellows program

The report also set out a proposed implementation schedule and probable costs.

Although the committee's report was approved by the board, a lag in implementation followed and led to the formation of another committee charged with developing a specific and detailed implementation strategy. Some steps were taken related to the long-range planning report—notably, to relinquish some land property, to reorganize the board committee structure and bylaws, to increase the frequency of board meetings, to strengthen financial discipline, and to redefine staff roles.

While the planning effort on the whole was comprehensive and thorough, it might have benefited from greater trustee involvement—they didn't "own" the planning effort—and a more direct focus on selected key issues.

Grand Canyon Association

In the minds of the board chair and executive of the Grand Canyon Association, the objective of the association's planning was simply to engage the board members more directly than before in the future of the association, and to have them recognize the need for more comprehensive planning, especially as it would effect a fundamental change in the mission. To that extent, the planning succeeded.

While no written report was made of the board's day-long retreat as the planning team, the results of the session, as set out in informal summaries by the executive director, were reviewed at the next board meeting and led to a determination to undertake a more comprehensive approach to planning that would address the mission change. Steps to strengthen the board were also a direct result of the planning.

Alzheimer's Association

The ad hoc governance planning work group functioned as the Alzheimer's Association's planning team, with the board itself not closely involved. Although the work group was part of the strategic planning exercise, it was concerned only with the governance and board development aspects. The issues were complex and sensitive, dealing with the board's size (sixty-five members), composition (part chapter representatives, part "public" members), and procedures (member recruitment and selection, and committee structure), as well as overall effectiveness.

After several meetings and conference calls to discuss memorandums related to various aspects of the problem, the work group held a two-day retreat, with the board chairman, the founding chairman, and the president in attendance. A preliminary report prepared by the discussion facilitator underwent extensive editing by the staff and was further revised by the work group in one other meeting and two conference calls before being submitted to the chapters for comment. While only modest changes were recommended and approved by the board, a corner was turned and steps got underway to improve board effectiveness and governance in general.

Grace Episcopal Church

The mission of a parish such as Grace Episcopal Church is clear enough, and the engagement of the parish's members and leaders is always of strategic importance. The day-long planning retreat produced lively and constructive discussion of major issues facing the parish. Although it would have been desirable, no written report of the session was prepared, and positive steps were put in motion. The vestry made a deliberate decision to undertake further, expanded planning before making any changes on matters identified in the retreat, and a follow-up retreat was scheduled. As direct outcomes of this initial planning, commitments were made, among other outcomes, to introduce a "generational change" in the parish outlook through changes in the composition of the vestry, and to review and intensify the parish fund raising and public relations efforts. The vestry believed that a new spirit had been engendered through the retreat planning process.

National Society of Fund Raising Executives, Washington, D.C., Chapter

Although all membership organizations, such as this chapter, exist to serve their members, many try as well to serve the public in some manner. For this reason, the Washington, D.C., chapter of the National Society of Fund Raising Executives sought through strategic planning to clarify its mission.

After two meetings, the planning team, composed of eight diversified chapter members, prepared a three-page memorandum report to the chapter's board. While reaffirming the chapter's mission, the report pointed to the need to emphasize the public service purposes of the chapter's activities in order to complement the underlying reason for its existence, to serve its members. Thus it recommended specifically strengthening the chapter's pro bono fund raising assistance to hard-pressed local organizations. The report was accepted by the chapter's board, and steps were taken to carry out its recommendations.

Gardner and Florence Call Cowles Foundation

The issue for the Gardner and Florence Call Cowles Foundation, a small, grant-making organization, was strategic and went to the heart of its mission: What would it do with its assets in the coming years?

The three-member planning team met twice and held two telephone conferences. It prepared a report calling for the foundation, at least for the time being, to stay its present course—that is, not to move toward termination but to continue to make disbursements beyond current income, with emphasis on grants to organizations in Iowa. The report was approved by the board. Strategic planning had served its purpose.

15

Action Steps
Conducting Strategic Planning

Once the planning organization and procedures have been determined and arrangements have been made, the planning team meets to conduct the actual planning. It proceeds in the following sequence:

1. *Mission.* The team reviews a current statement of the mission, identifying questions and disagreements on matters of purpose and values, without seeking to resolve differences, which will be the outcome of the planning session.

2. *External environment.* The team spends time speculating on demographic, political, economic, and other trends, seeking to identify *opportunities* and *threats* (obstacles) to its programs.

3. *Internal environment.* The team then turns to its own organization, identifying its *strengths* and its *weaknesses* as it seeks to fulfill its mission and faces the external environment.

4. *Critical issues.* In a taxing exercise, the team selects the issues that will be most important for the future of the organization (probably no fewer than three but no more than seven).

5. *Deliberation.* For each critical issue, the team assigns a breakout group to prepare recommendations; or the planning team as a whole discusses in detail each issue, being sure to have in

mind the opportunities and threats and the strengths and
weaknesses as it proposes realistic solutions, not just hopes
and dreams.

6. *Outcome*. The planning team agrees on a reaffirmation or
   modification of the mission and an expression of the vision
   of what the organization will be and do in the coming years—
   its direction and priorities.

7. *Report*. The team assigns responsibility for drafting a report to
   be reviewed at a later time and then approved by the board.

Taking each of these action steps presents a strong challenge to
the planning team. The team must not underestimate the substantive importance of each step in the logical progression in giving
solidity to the final step, the report. On the other hand, the team
should constantly bear in mind that it will have met the challenge
if it can give clear expression to its views, setting out a realistic
vision; it should not think at this point in the planning procedure
that it must produce a polished, comprehensive strategic plan.

Part IV

From Planning to Action

The major part, the substance and core, of strategic planning has been achieved when the board and planning team have followed the rigorous path to create the report. It is then a matter of translating the "architect's drawing" into practical, usable blueprints, instruments to guide the organization. Such guiding instruments take two forms: the *strategic plan* and *operational plans*.

The strategic plan, discussed at length in Chapter Sixteen, fills out the planning team's report, articulating in greater detail the mission, the vision, and the direction that programs will take to fulfill that vision. It serves as a clearly defined guide for both board and staff. Operational plans, discussed in Chapter Seventeen, can be drawn up to guide the day-to-day activities of the organization in implementing the strategic plan. In Chapter Eighteen, the steps the board must take to complete the planning effort are described.

16

Putting Together the Strategic Plan

The progression from vision to strategic plan, from the report of the planning team to a useful plan, is a matter of practicality. The planning team cannot be expected to formulate a comprehensive, fully edited plan in its sessions. It can set the direction, a pattern, and a framework of priorities on the basis of which drafters—staff or board members or a combination of the two—can prepare a full strategic plan.

The planning team and the board will want to approve the strategic plan because it will spell out in more detail the mission and the changes that the planning team has recommended should govern the organization henceforth. Some people may say, "When you are done with planning sessions, you can forget the strategic plan. The basic purpose has been achieved in getting the leaders to think strategically; the plan will only gather dust on the shelf."

But a strategic plan can serve several important purposes. Once it has been reviewed and formally approved by the board, the document will provide the organization's mission with the stature it needs. It will set out an unequivocal base for implementation steps, both programmatic and administrative, including budget determinations, staff assignments, and committee direction. None of these activities can be adequately based on only the report of the planning sessions.

Moreover, a strategic plan will put on record criteria, or benchmarks, against which to evaluate performance on each direction in which the board has determined the organization should proceed. The plan will have inherently set the framework for the staff and the board to look back in a year's time to evaluate progress.

In terms of fund raising, the strategic plan will be the reliable base for determining funding needs, and for making the case for support of a particular program.

Strategic plans need not be long, but they also should not be too brief. Several elements not necessarily included in the report of the planning sessions but flowing from it can be set out. For example:

- A management structure, possibly a new alignment of programs or chapters, can be prescribed.

- Governance arrangements and changes in board organization, procedures, or activities can be laid out.

- Plans to build any new facilities—always major determinations—can be spelled out.

- The rationale and lines of an adjusted public image can be described.

The format of a strategic plan, while in many ways comparable to the report of the planning sessions, can follow a precise outline, one that the steering committee and the planning team have agreed upon in advance. A likely outline for a strategic plan would be the following:

An Executive Summary

1. A reaffirmation of the mission, with any adjustments

2. A summary of the significant external and internal environmental factors that influence the plan

3. The critical issues on which the plan focuses
4. The elements of the plan, oriented to the critical issues:
    a. Program determinations
    b. Priorities
    c. Management determinations—personnel, funding, and so on
    d. Governance determinations: board organizations and procedures

Once it has been approved by the board, the strategic plan can be turned over to the staff to prepare the operational plans, described in Chapter Seventeen. Even as the distinction needs to be clear between the report of the planning sessions and the strategic plan, so it is especially important to make a deliberate distinction between the mission and vision, which belong in the strategic plan, and implementation matters, which should be left to the operational plans.

17

Creating Operational Plans

The chief executive is charged with translating the strategic plan into reality, with seeing that it is implemented. This is done through *operational plans*.

In the normal course of events, managers periodically prepare plans for the programs and projects for which they are responsible. With a strategic plan in place, operational plans take on an increased importance. They show how programs and projects will be changed. They set up criteria against which to evaluate performance, to weigh achievement in fulfilling the strategic plan.

Operational plans can follow many different forms. The following pattern, which has proved reliable, provides a simple, standard outline that can apply to any program or project. Using the same format for all programs and projects—whether substantive, operational, or administrative; large or small; short- or long-term—allows for comparability. Succinctness is of premium importance; there should be no padding. If you want board members to be interested, your operational programs will be short and direct.

Operational Plan

1. Subject (or overall purpose): one sentence at most
2. Present status: what has been achieved (quantified where appropriate)

3. Proposed courses of action: specific new or reenforcing actions for reaching different or greater purposes (including meeting strategic plan directives)

4. Targets of achievement: specific points (quantified where appropriate), including timing

5. Administration: Who takes action? What personnel and funding are needed?

The operational plan for a single program or project should fit on one double-spaced typed page. The operational plan for the whole organization will be the assemblage of the separate one-page program and project plans.

Operational plans are a tool of management, but the executive probably will want the board to approve any plans. Board committees will find operational plans helpful in filling their oversight roles.

18

Action Steps
Strategic and Operational Plans

When the planning team and the board have approved the report of the planning sessions, the board makes sure that steps are taken to complete the planning effort. The report of the planning team should be clear on the vision and the direction the organization is to go; it cannot be expected to be a comprehensive document that can guide the organization in the years to come. There is still need for a polished strategic plan and for operational plans to implement the strategic plan.

The board takes the following steps in sequence:

1. *Development of the strategic plan:* The board designates the steering committee, assisted by staff, to prepare for the board's approval a strategic plan that elaborates more formally and comprehensively on the report of the planning sessions.

2. *Preparation of operational plans:* After the board approves the strategic plan, the board asks the chief executive to prepare operational plans for the implementation of the strategic plan, which at the board's discretion can be reviewed and approved by board committees or the board itself.

3. *Conduct of periodic reviews:* The board determines at what intervals and by what methods it or its committees will revisit

the strategic plan to evaluate performance and when
another full-scale or partial strategic planning exercise
should be undertaken.

Strategic plans run the risk of being lengthy, too detailed, and
full of fluff. They need not be. If they give precision to the report
of the planning sessions and are practical in terms of recognizing
obstacles to achievement, they can be a firm base for operational
plans and themselves be used as a constant point of reference. Similarly, the operational plans to implement the strategic plan, if
drawn up along practical lines, will serve the organization well as
guideposts of its programs and a benchmark against which to evaluate performance.

Part V

Keys to Successful Planning

The process of strategic planning—preparing and conducting planning activities—can be summarized in terms of a few underlying principles, which are presented in Chapter Nineteen. Organizations undertaking strategic planning are well advised to pay special attention to two aspects in particular: readiness to proceed down the planning path, and making the effort worthwhile. Chapter Twenty offers final tips for the planning process.

19

Principles of Successful Planning

Successful strategic planning is achieved when the following principles are adhered to:

1. The overriding purpose of strategic planning is not to write a beautiful plan—though a good strategic plan can be helpful in the board's governance, in the executive's management, in fund raising, and in performance evaluation—but rather to get the organization to think strategically, to set sights and not be consumed with this year's budget or that foundation's grant.

2. Strategic planning is quintessentially for the board. Only the board can determine what the organization will be and do in the next five to ten years; only the board can stand by the values and set the course. It is the board that must *own* the strategic planning process and outcomes. Strategic planning loses all meaning if it is turned over to the staff, to a committee, or to an outside consultant.

3. Accordingly, the board itself should take full responsibility for the planning. If the full board does not itself do the planning, it should establish the procedures, especially the composition of the planning team, of which board leaders should be members, and it should approve the resulting strategic plan.

4. To place responsibility for strategic planning squarely on the board is by no means to exclude the executive and staff. The initiative to undertake the planning will often and appropriately come

from the executive. Once the planning is undertaken, the bulk of support for the board or planning team will fall to the staff. On the other hand, while staff members may participate as members of the planning team, they should not dominate the discussions.

5.   The board will want to appoint a steering committee to prepare for the planning, to make plans for planning, to recommend the organization and procedures to be followed, leaving the conduct of the planning, the substance, to the board or the planning team. There is much for such a steering committee to do, assisted by staff, to making the planning activities effective: determining the composition of the planning team; making the arrangements for planning sessions, including whether to hold a retreat; preparing the materials to have available; and deciding whether to retain a consultant or discussion leader.

6.   Marshaling constituency views may be important: arrangements may need to be made to include representatives—such as beneficiaries, donors, and staff—on the planning team; to undertake surveys or interviews; or to hold focus group meetings to ensure constituent input in the planning. The essence of planning, however, is in the planning sessions; preparing too much material for those sessions can be wasteful and diversionary. Endless data won't produce good board evaluations, and predigested recommendations can only reduce board involvement.

7.   Board involvement and board ownership cannot be achieved by trying to do strategic planning in regular board meetings. For effective planning, special meetings, preferably off-site, are needed.

8.   An outside professional consultant or discussion leader can make a difference. A consultant can advise on the many and important arrangements. As moderator or facilitator, the discussion leader will be outcome driven, allowing the chair as a full participant to express views instead of leading the discussion. As the outsider, the moderator can play devil's advocate, forcing participants to look beneath matters easily taken for granted.

9.   Probably the most difficult part of the strategic planning process is for the board or planning team to settle on the key issues—maybe three or four but not more than six or seven. The focus must first be on ends—what the organization wants to achieve—and then on an exploration of the means—what programs or changes are needed to achieve the ends. The central focus of strategic planning can only be reached through intense discussion by the planning team; it cannot be determined by staff, a committee, or a consultant.

10.   The outcome of planning sessions is a report that reaffirms or modifies the organization's mission and sets out its vision, purpose, and priorities, particularly with respect to the ends to be achieved and the means to achieve those ends; this report can be the basis of a strategic plan.

11.   The strategic plan, more formal and comprehensive than the report of the planning team, is separately drawn up for board approval.

12.   Operational plans, the details of programs for implementing the strategic plan, are prepared by the staff.

Principles are not designed to simplify the process. They should offer guides to achieving success in what is never an easy activity, and perhaps some cautions to assist in avoiding pitfalls.

20

Final Tips

The previous chapter summarizes the basic principles of strategic planning—the approach, the preparation for strategic planning, the conduct of strategic planning, and the end product. Board members and executives are often plagued, however, by two general questions: *What are the signs that show that an organization is ready to undertake strategic planning or to repeat the process?* and *What keeps a strategic plan vital and useful?*

Readiness

It may be time for strategic planning when conditions change; when internal or external circumstances bring into question the organization's mission; when programs are dropped or new dimensions are added; when the organization joins other organizations; when funders, such as foundations, corporations, United Ways, and regular annual supporters, show signs of lagging interest; when board members begin to raise doubts about the effectiveness of programs or personnel; when the old strategic plan begins to look a little stale; when in the passage of time, new board members and perhaps key staff have come on board; and when new involvement and a fresh outlook are needed.

Some organizations have a standing planning committee that is charged not to plan but to keep watch over performance under existing plans on behalf of the board and to be aware of the need for a renewed planning effort. Such a committee can keep the board focused on planning and on the timeliness of another full effort. There is no fast rule, but a good executive and a lively board will know when it is time.

Vitality

A strategic plan that is not too long, that avoids clichés and bland generalizations, and that tackles the key issues is the best insurance against its gathering dust on the shelf.

Successful planning will have gotten the organization to think strategically. That in itself will help to ensure the board's continuing attention to the mission and to the vision of what it wants the organization to be and do. A plan that has within it the design for regular review, and a board that follows through, will keep strategic planning from being a wasted effort. A conscientious executive helps.

In the end, strategic planning is only as useful as the board makes it.

Resources

Resources

Resource A
Often-Heard Objections to Strategic Planning

Four objections to strategic planning and to plans for planning are often raised by board members or the executive:

1. *"We are too busy getting on with the programs to take time out to indulge in planning."* If strategic planning is undertaken at the most only every three or four years, it can be carried out without undue interference with day-to-day operations. When a board itself has the will to devote the time necessary to undertake the planning, the organization is better off because of the demonstrable commitment of its leaders.

2. *"We have an effective committee system; why not use it?"* Strategic planning far transcends the mandate of any one committee and is altogether different from the other matters that come before a board, matters that committees can explore and then recommend policies and actions to the board. Moreover, planning is not a matter of approving policy lines drawn up by a committee; rather, it is an expression of fundamental purposes—the vision of what the organization will be and do in the coming years. It is quite appropriate and advantageous for a board to appoint a committee to make plans for planning, but not a standing committee to do the actual planning. A steering committee will involve itself in devising the planning organization and procedures—when and how the planning should take place—but not in the substance of planning.

3. *"The board is too big to be effective in planning."* There is no reason why a board of twenty or even thirty, with proper arrangements and expertly led, cannot be fully effective in planning. If the board is larger or there is need to involve many others in the process, boards can select a planning team—those who will actually do the planning—that includes key board members who command the respect of the whole organization. And the board can closely watch over the team's deliberations and ultimately approve its product.

4. *"Our board won't be bothered with strategic planning."* If members of the board are indifferent, or simply won't accept the need or desirability for strategic planning, there may be no solution other than to work toward a change in board composition, to recruit new blood. One step, however, may be effective in changing some minds: invite to a board discussion a board member from another organization that has had a successful experience with strategic planning, or a planning consultant who can explain the process and discuss its value. A friendly outsider may be able to show that strategic planning need not be too burdensome and may be just what the organization needs.

An organization seeking the help of a consultant in its strategic planning will need to select the elements of planning on which it wishes to receive assistance. A comprehensive consulting plan might include the following steps, roughly in order of priority. (*Note:* an approximation of the number of *consultancy days* required for each element is indicated. The time estimates are inescapably variable, however, depending on the experience and needs of the organization.

Moreover, on such steps as obtaining constituency views, if the consultant is to advise but not take an active part in the interviews or focus group meetings, considerably less time will be needed. The time allotted for leading the sessions will depend directly on how many days of planning sessions and retreat are planned for or indeed actually take place, which may be determined only as the planning proceeds.)

1. Assisting the steering committee in making recommendations to the board on the preparations for planning (five days):
   a. Determining the composition of the planning team
   b. Making arrangements for the planning sessions or retreat, place, meals, facilities, and so on

      c. Marshaling needed materials—history, previous planning, current and projected programs, finances, fund raising, associated and competitive organizations, and so on (constituency views are separate)

      d. Preparing a questionnaire for the planning team in anticipation of planning sessions or retreat

2. Advising on or participating in obtaining constituency views through surveys, interviews, or focus group meetings (five days)

3. Leading the planning sessions or retreat as facilitator (two to three days)

4. Overseeing and guiding the preparation of the report of the planning sessions or retreat (two days)

5. Assisting the planning team in presenting results to the board (one day)

6. Overseeing and guiding the preparation of the strategic plan (two days)

7. Overseeing and guiding the preparation of operational plans to implement the strategic plan (two days)

References

American Association of Museums. *Excellence and Equity*. Washington, D.C.: American Association of Museums, 1992.

Barry, B. W. *Strategic Planning Workbook for Nonprofit Organizations*. St. Paul, Minn.: Amherst H. Wilder Foundation, 1996.

Bryson, J. M. *Strategic Planning for Public and Nonprofit Organizations: A Guide to Strengthening and Sustaining Organizational Achievement*. San Francisco: Jossey-Bass, 1988.

Carver, J. *Boards That Make a Difference: A New Design for Leadership in Nonprofit and Public Organizations*. San Francisco: Jossey-Bass, 1990.

Collins, J. C., and Porras, J. I. *Built to Last: Successful Habits of Visionary Companies*. New York: HarperCollins, 1994.

Cook, J. B. *Planning for Nonprofit Organizations: Defining Purpose*. San Francisco: Support Centers of America, 1987.

Drucker, P. F. *Managing the Nonprofit Organization*. New York: HarperCollins, 1990.

Eadie, D. C. *Beyond Strategic Planning: How to Involve Nonprofit Boards in Growth and Change*. Booklet. Washington, D.C.: National Center for Nonprofit Boards, 1993.

Greene, D. *Planning for Nonprofit Organizations: Creating a Vision as Part of a Strategic Plan*. San Francisco: Support Centers of America, 1988.

Hodgkin, C. "Policy and Paperclips: Rejecting the Lure of the Corporate Model." *Nonprofit Management and Leadership*, Summer 1993.

Howe, F. "What You Need to Know About Fund Raising." *Harvard Business Review*, Mar./Apr. 1985.

Howe, F. "Fund Raising and the Nonprofit Board Member." Booklet no. 3. Washington, D.C.: National Center for Nonprofit Boards, 1988.

Howe, F. *The Board Member's Guide to Fund Raising: What Every Trustee Needs to Know About Raising Money.* San Francisco: Jossey-Bass, 1991.

Howe, F. *Welcome to the Board: Your Guide to Effective Participation.* San Francisco: Jossey-Bass, 1995.

O'Connor, P. T. "On Language." *The New York Times Magazine*, August 27, 1995.

O'Harrow, H. Jr., and Lipton, E. "George Mason Embroiled in Debate About Its Mission." *The Washington Post*, Feb. 14, 1996.

National Society of Fund Raising Executives. *Long-Range Plan: 1994–1998.* Washington, D.C.: National Society of Fund Raising Executives, 1993.

Park, D. G. Jr. Strategic Planning and the Nonprofit Board. Booklet no. 6, Governance Series. Washington, D.C.: National Center for Nonprofit Boards, 1990.

Relic, P. D. *Remarks to the Faculty.* Bulletin. North Shore Country Day School, Winnetka, Ill., 1995.

Stoesz, E., and Raber, C. *Doing Good Better! How to Be an Effective Board Member of a Nonprofit Organization.* Intercourse, Penn.: Good Books, 1994.

Szanton, P. *Board Assessment of the Organization: How Are We Doing?* Booklet no. 14, Governance Series. Washington, D.C.: National Center for Nonprofit Boards, 1992.

Wickenden, J. *Independent Thinking.* Bulletin. Princeton, N.J.: Wickenden Associates, July 1995.

Index